PRAISE FOR

'There is much in *Let it Be* that fit… …uctive
Living. I applaud this he… …k.

- David K. Reynolds, Developer of Constructive Living and noted authority on Japanese Psychotherapy

'Graham Old has long been one of my favorite hypnotists and writers. The ideas in this book draw from proven therapeutic modalities, and this book makes these ideas accessible, powerful, and practical. Those who benefit from these ideas will find much sought-after relief from suffering.'

- Dr. Richard Nongard, Author of *The Self-Hypnosis Solution*

'Properly understood and practised acceptance is one of the most reliable positive pathways of change known in all of psychological science. Acceptance is not tolerance, resignation, or giving up. It is receiving the hard earned gift of your own experience. If you are suffering you need a pathway forward, but more of the same will not give you what you yearn for. Stop running; plant your feet; and pick up this gentle book. It will take you by the hand and show you a powerful new pathway toward what you really want.'

- Steven C. Hayes, Originator of Acceptance and Commitment Therapy and author of *A Liberated Mind*

Let it Be

Let it Be

Graham Old

How Acceptance Can Liberate You
to Live the Life You Love

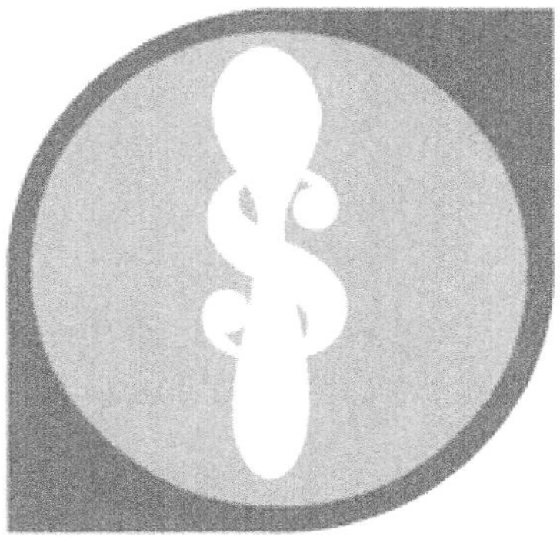

Let it Be – How Acceptance Can Liberate You to Live the Life You Love

Published 2021 by Plastic Spoon

ISBN 978-1-8384000-0-2

www.plasticspoonbooks.com

Portions of Chapter 8 and Chapter 13 were originally published in *The Anxiety Guide*.

Acknowledgements

I am grateful to Richard Nongard for his many years of support and for his tireless efforts to promote contextual psychology in arenas where it has not traditionally been acknowledged.

Heartfelt thanks go to those brave clients of mine who agreed to share aspects of their story with the reader.

Disclaimer

Please be aware that any experimentation with the ideas presented in this book is undertaken at your own risk and responsibility. Nothing in this book should be taken as a replacement for seeking professional psychological or medical support.

Also by Graham Old

Fiction

Of Madness and Folly

Non-fiction

Mastering the Leisure Induction

Revisiting Hypnosis

The Elman Induction

The Hypnotic Handshakes

My Friend John

Hypnosis with the Hard to Hypnotise

Therapeutic Inductions

The Anxiety Guide

Use Hypnosis to Stop Smoking

Use Hypnosis to Overcome Blushing

Memory Tools

Preface

This is the second book in the '*Self Help for the Rest of us*' series of books. This series aims to demystify the whole area of personal development, emotional well-being and self-help.

None of the books in the '*Self Help for the Rest of us*' series are written by people who have arrived, or who are considered enlightened gurus or self-help celebrities. Nothing contained within our books is presented as absolute fact, or unquestionable instructions. Instead, we are aiming to provide perspectives to consider, approaches to explore and solutions to experiment with. The 'truth' of anything written in these pages is purely pragmatic. (That is, does it work for you?)

I am not a naturally serene type of person. When I was a child, I was told that I was "a worrier." I was not aware of it at the time, but enough people have since confirmed it that I suppose it could very well have been true. In my late teens, it would be fair to say that I was constantly angry, actively seeking out situations where I could explode and pass on the angst I was feeling inside to anyone and everyone around me.

There are whole segments of my life where I barely functioned, locked in a dark cell of depression. I could go on with my story, but it would not include what many "look at me now" accounts tend to promote. I did not have any blinding moments of revelation. There were no epiphanies or instant transformations. I never reached enlightenment and I was not bestowed with any special insights, or secret truths.

I remain a work in progress, as we all do. However, I reached a point where I had to accept that cynically dismissing every piece of advice I encountered was not getting me anywhere. So, I began systematically experimenting and road-testing various therapeutic or self-help tools, rejecting those that did not work for me and passionately pursuing those which showed promising results.

It was years later that I realised that the methods that had worked for me appeared to have the same central idea at their core: acceptance. *Let it Be* is the result of years of testing these methods, both by myself and by those who would later come to see me for therapy or coaching.

This book – built upon evidence-based psychological approaches, as well as popular self-help methods – does not intend to promise you a life of bliss. In my opinion, it offers you more. It aims to help you lead a productive and fulfilling life, despite the existence of unpleasant emotions, or unwanted experiences. If you are ready and willing to road-test the ideas contained in this book, it offers you an opportunity to live the life you love, in the here and now.

All clients' names have been changed to preserve anonymity.

Contents

Introduction

This book introduces the idea and practice of Brief Acceptance. This is a collective term for a series of useful therapies, self-help tools, ideas or techniques which share a common core: acceptance.

The first half of the book will discuss ideas and exercises from various therapy models that utilise acceptance. However, this is not a heavy academic discussion. Instead, I have drawn out practical and beneficial content from the different therapeutic approaches and show you how to apply it in your life.

The second half of the book looks at self-help strategies that promote acceptance. There are no pseudo-scientific or supposedly spiritual claims made here. Instead, the strategies we will look at have been pragmatically chosen, based on their positive track-record in assisting people to live more fulfilled lives due to their acceptance-based methods.

Which Methods are Included?

We have done our best not to exclude any therapies, tools or techniques which may be useful. The primary inclusion criteria is simply a focus on acceptance as the key to moving beyond 'problems' and into life.

So, we include the following recognised psychotherapeutic models:

- Acceptance and Commitment Therapy
- Dialectical Behaviour Therapy
- Mindfulness Based Stress Reduction
- Morita Therapy

Yet, we also use the term to refer to self-help or complementary therapy strategies, including:

- The Work

- The Option Method
- The Emotional Freedom Technique

It would be fair to say that we are using the term *Brief Acceptance* to refer to a mindset or an orientation, rather than to describe specific approaches.

So, What is *not* Included?

Brief Acceptance is not a "closed church." That is, you would not find us providing an exclusive list of what does count as Brief Acceptance and what does not. Having said that, there are some schools of thought that we have taken the decision *not* to focus on.

We do not discuss religions or models that have a predominantly 'spiritual' focus. This is primarily because our aim is not to discover *the meaning of life* or dictate any *absolute truths*. So, any approaches that move beyond acceptance to focus on the purpose of life, spiritual *bliss* or 'higher consciousness' will be avoided.

In some cases, it has been difficult to know where to draw the line. After all, there is much in Buddhism and various schools of Hinduism that speaks of acceptance. And, although we have included *The*

Work and *The Option Method*, the developers of such systems have at times used their tools as stepping-stones to explore some of the 'big questions' of life. That is where our discussion of them ends.

To avoid unnecessary controversy or distracting debates, our focus remains fixed on acceptance. We believe it is possible to employ acceptance for ourselves and others to find greater levels of contentment and happiness in life. And we would argue that this is possible regardless of any religious or spiritual commitments.

This is a Practical Book!

This is not an academic book. Numerous aspects of it are based on academic research, or at least backed-up by it. I am something of a research geek and love reading about all of that. However, I recognise that not everyone thinks like me! So, I have sought to take the theoretical elements and demonstrate their practical application.

Let it Be is not intended to merely give you ideas to think about, or theories to discuss. The whole aim of this book is to empower you to actively live the life you love, despite any setbacks, obstacles or difficulties. So, it would be more than a little bit ironic if the book itself was more theoretical than practical! Therefore, as you prepare to dive into the world of Brief Acceptance, I hope you are ready to get your hands dirty.

CHAPTER ONE

The Constant Struggle

Does it ever feel as if Life is just one battle after another?

I'm sure that we have all felt like that at different times in our lives. It might be the persistent battles with family or colleagues, or the struggle to drag yourself out of bed in the morning when you can think of a hundred reasons not to. It may just be the ongoing task of finding a way to make your money last until the end of the month.

Then there are the deeper battles—the ones that feel

like they're almost a part of us, showing no signs of ever going away. I'm thinking of things like the struggle for self-acceptance, the challenge of coming to terms with our past experiences, or the battle with daily resentment over our position in life, knowing that we deserve more and have worked harder than this.

All of these struggles have one significant thing in common—they all require us to fight against reality. The world—or at least our experience of the world, our life—has not turned out the way we thought it should. And we cannot stand that. These experiences can vary enormously. Perhaps we're not happy that our grandparents died in our childhood. Or maybe we resent our friends for being more successful than us. Or we might not be able to get past traumatic events we've experienced. Maybe we begrudge some of the physical features we were born with. The nature of our battles varies from person to person.

At first, it may seem as if a 'fight against reality' is a foolish thing and clearly a fruitless battle. However, when you consider the nature of the experiences we're railing against, it can also be incredibly enticing and even seem like the only reasonable response. There's just one tiny niggling problem with that—there's nothing at all reasonable about arguing with reality.

You are never going to win.

***

Lucy had wanted to be a professional singer for as long as she could remember. Opera, West End Musicals, lead singer in a chart-topping rock n' roll band—she didn't care where she would be singing, as long as she did.

Lucy shone in the school choir. She was the star of all school performances and was often asked to assist the teachers with some of the other pupils who were struggling.

When it came to College, Lucy predictably went down the Drama route. This meant more demanding roles, but she was not deterred. She considered it good preparation for the West End.

Lucy sang from the moment she got up, until the moment her first lesson began. She attended choir at lunchtime and was even allowed to join the Orchestra, with her voice as her instrument. The minute College was over, Lucy sang all the way home and barely stopped until she went to sleep.

Singing was Lucy's life, and—if everything went according to plan—it was also her future. And her future looked bright.

Today, aged 28, Lucy works in Property. She is the Assistant Letting Manager for a local Estate Agent, securing suitable apartments for the successful Londoners who can afford them. She no longer sings.

When watching TV talent shows, Lucy has been known to shed a tear or two, remembering the dreams she once held dear. She listens to music constantly—much to her family's annoyance—but she no longer sings along.

I met Lucy through a mutual friend. She found out that I was about to begin my training in hypnosis and asked if it would be able to help her. I asked what she wanted help with, and her eyes welled-up immediately.

"Everything," she said. "Everything. I need help with me, *if I'm honest. I'm just so angry. So damn resentful. And I can't get beyond it. I just can't stop obsessing over it."*

***

I wish I knew back then what I know today about the power of acceptance. Not only do I think it could have turned Lucy's life around, but it would have been incredibly beneficial for me too. And now—as you stick around and implement the lessons in this book—it could also be genuinely life-changing for you.

Learning how and why to stop focusing on the past, or attempting to remedy anything and everything in your life that is unpleasant, may be precisely the solution you need for those daily battles you face.

It turns out that laying down your sword may actually win you the war!

***

Eli's wife left him on their 10th Wedding Anniversary. She moved in with his brother, with whom she had been having an affair for over 2 years. She took their young daughter with her, claiming that Eli's brother was the biological father (a claim that Eli later found out was untrue).

As he describes it, Eli's life fell apart. He got drunk the night his wife left, and most nights after that. He started taking repeated sick days off work. After a while, he wouldn't even offer an excuse. He would just ring his boss and say, "Can't do it. I can't come in today."

Eventually, Eli lost his job and lacked the motivation to look for another one. He was placed on anti-depressants by his doctor, but by now his life had lost all routine and he rarely remembered to take them. He began claiming benefits and relied on food banks to give him anything close to a healthy diet.

It was one day when he was visiting the food bank

that an elderly volunteer asked Eli if he liked to read. He said that he used to but had no energy for it any more. The old woman showed Eli a fairly slim book she had just finished reading, suggesting it wouldn't take much energy to get through.

Eli shrugged his shoulders, and the woman placed the book in with his food items. She asked him to donate it to a library or charity shop if he didn't enjoy as much as she thought he would.

The book was Constructive Living *by David Reynolds, and one of its main lessons—derived from Morita Therapy, which we will look at later—is that we can learn to accept our unpleasant feelings and experience life 'as it is.'*

Eli read the book three times. The first time, he was so disgusted by the unrealistic and naive ideas it contained that he threw it in the bin. The next day, having woken-up in a dreadful mood, he took the book out of the bin, intending to go through it with a red pen, refuting it page by page. As it turned-out, this time, he had more questions than objections. He wrote questions, comments, and ideas on almost every page. The ideas still seemed unrealistic to him, and he did put a line through one or two paragraphs, but the whole thing was somehow more intriguing to him now. He felt, for the first time in a long while, a vague sense of something like hope.

The third time Eli read Constructive Living, *he did so with an inquisitive mind. He was ready to see if the lessons it contained could be realistically applied in his life. That was the day that everything changed.*

Eli learned that although he could not be held responsible for his feelings—which he could not directly change—he was still responsible for his actions. He discovered that he could learn to accept his feelings as they were and that every feeling, no matter how unpleasant, can be useful.

The more he read, the more Eli felt his objections and excuses fading away. He decided there and then to take charge of his life and to make the most of whatever came his way. There would be ups and downs, of course, but Eli felt like he had a new purpose in life, and that kept him moving forward.

His life was not transformed over night, but years later, he would look back at the day he read the book with an open and inquisitive mind as the day his transformation began.

***

Over the last 20 years, I have been privileged to work with people like Eli a number of times. In my work with families and individuals—employing both solution-focused brief therapy and hypnosis—I have encountered situations time and again where resentment, guilt, anger, fear, shame, anxiety, and depression have been daily companions for people. Just getting out of bed for some people can feel like a real battle. It is a battle they may win more often than not, but it will be waiting for them the following morning. And the one after that. Perhaps you can empathise with the level of exhaustion such daily struggles can bring?

I work with a number of people on the autism spectrum, and anxiety is a common complaint in my clinic. I learned early on that the worst thing someone can do about anxiety is worry about it. It sounds simple, almost banal to state that, yet it turns out that it is highly significant. People who have anxiety disorders are very often characterised by a tendency to worry about being worried. However, this is also true of a whole host of issues.

Those struggling with uncontrollable blushing often blush because they are nervous about blushing. Those who have panic attacks are very often literally panicking at the thought of a panic attack. Someone with stage fright may freeze or fumble because they are concerned about doing precisely that. This same kind of self-fulfilling prophecy is seen time and time again.

In my clinical practice, I started to use mindfulness

with such clients. Before I knew it, I was teaching various mindfulness skills to almost every single client I knew. And then it hit me.

My clients came to see me with issues that were made far worse due to their desire (and attempts) to avoid those issues. Their determination to avoid any and all unpleasant experiences almost guaranteed that they would experience them.

Armed with this insight, I returned to my books. I listened more closely to my clients, and I committed to keeping an open mind to any other lessons I had missed. I soon realised, with more than a little excitement, that almost every issue I encountered involved an impossible battle with reality. I also saw—and could not believe I had never seen it before—that practically every effective therapeutic method I revisited contained some element of acceptance.

I devoted myself to the topic of acceptance, learning to embrace life as it is, making it a core component of my therapeutic work. I am now an author, trainer, and speaker on all aspects of hypnosis and emotional well-being. The power of acceptance—especially what I have come to call 'Brief Acceptance'—is something that I never tire of sharing.

Rarely have I been confident of anything more than

this: if you commit yourself with an open mind to learning *and practising* the principles in this book, you will see true transformation in your life. I cannot promise that you will not have any more problems. However, I *can* tell you that your problems will have less of an impact on your life and that nothing will be able to hold you back from living your life with purpose.

In the pages that follow, I will share various techniques for implementing acceptance in your life. I will address some of the more common objections to a life of acceptance and provide practical lessons and exercises for you to learn from.

If such lessons sound desirable to you, I encourage you to keep reading. More than that, I strongly encourage you to go through the exercises and lessons contained in this book.

As you do so, I am confident that you will begin to experience the power of acceptance and learn to refocus on the life you desire, no longer stalled by unpleasant experiences or feelings. You will find yourself designing a life that you value and working toward it, not ruminating over your past, your perceived inadequacies, or your unwanted feelings.

In the following chapter, we will explain exactly what we mean by 'acceptance' and 'Brief Acceptance.' Keep reading to discover one of the most powerful and simple tools you might ever encounter.

CHAPTER TWO

What is Brief Acceptance?

'We must accept the absolutely unchangeable to change the absolutely unacceptable.'[1]

If all of this talk of Acceptance is new to you, I understand that it could seem a little idealistic, naïve, and of no actual help in the real world. However, I would ask you to lend me your trust, just for the length of this book.

I was completely serious and sincere in the last chapter when I said that the power of acceptance

1 Ogawa, *A River to Live By*, p. 68.

changed my life. More than that, I see it transform lives weekly in my clinic. It would not be unfair to say that the only clients I have had that it has not been of help to are those who have been unwilling to try it out.

I invite you to read this chapter and the rest of this book with an attitude of curiosity. You do not need to buy-in to every single thing I say before deciding to give it a go. Yet, you will need to be willing to road-test the ideas and lessons you will find here. This is by no means a theoretical book!

***

Thirty years before she walked into my clinic, Margaret had been sat beside her husband's hospital bed, holding his hand. She had been there almost constantly for the previous two weeks, unable to leave her David on his own.

The nurses on the ward were worried for Margaret, as it was evident that her visits to the hospital and the hours she sat beside her husband's bed were taking their toll on her. They finally managed to convince her to take a day off, to stay at home and rest. That was the day that David passed away.

Margaret was one-hundred and one years old when she came to see me. For thirty years, she had carried the burden of feeling like she had failed her husband. However, that feeling spread as the years went on, and by the time we met, Margaret said that she hated every moment of every day. She felt unable to accept David's death, or to forgive herself for not being there at the end. She felt as if everything was wrong in the world and inwardly complained about almost everything—the weather was wrong, her neighbours were too noisy, her mattress was uncomfortable, there were too many cars parked in her street, the birds were singing at the wrong pitch, her skin was too saggy, there was never anything good on TV, her grandchildren did not visit often enough, her children visited too often, and on and on...

Margaret had learned how to look and sound positive. She simply had to remember how she had been for the first 71 years of her life. However, she was fighting a daily battle with reality every moment of every day.

In our first session, after Margaret had talked about David's death and her daily struggles to see anything good in the world, she looked up at me and said, "I'm just so tired."

***

Maybe you can relate to Margaret? Perhaps the notion of battling with reality captures aspects of how you currently go through life. If so, I am sure you know just how exhausting the constant struggle can be. The good news is that there is another option. That alternative is what we have come to call *Brief Acceptance*.

What is Acceptance?

So, what exactly do we mean by acceptance? As we use the term in this book, we are talking about the complete acceptance of life *as it is*.

That means accepting:

- When things do not go according to plan
- Yourself
- Your body
- Your feelings
- Past experiences
- Your job
- Your family
- The actions of others
- Your sex-life

- Your financial situation
- How your life turned out
- The state of the world

In short, we are talking about accepting reality as we encounter it. This does not mean we never take action to change things, as we will see later. However, this present moment—and your past experience—cannot be any different than it is. Wishing it was otherwise is simply an act of denial.

You may as well get upset that your cat does not bark, or complain that your pear tree doesn't produce apples. It simply is the way that it is.

Acceptance is the active choice to allow unpleasant experiences—past and present—to exist, without trying to deny or avoid them. After all, what else can we really do?

It turns out that the effort we put into avoiding suffering, pain, and the struggles of life is only the cause of more suffering and more pain and becomes yet another struggle. The insistence on only having positive experiences is therefore in itself a negative experience.[2]

By contrast, acceptance means acknowledging and

2 Cf. Manson, *The subtle art of not giving a fuck*, pp. 9-11.

making room for unpleasant experiences, painful feelings, sensations, urges, and emotions. We drop the struggle with them and allow them to be as they are. Instead of fighting them, resisting them, running from them, or getting overwhelmed by them, we let them be.

You may wonder if such an attitude would simply make you a passive observer of life. After all, is dissatisfaction with the way things are not the key to action? I would argue the exact opposite. Acceptance of things the way they are is actually a key requirement for taking action. For example, which of the following statements sounds more active?

1) *"I can't stand the idea that I've been burgled! I can't believe it. I wish it hadn't happened."*

2) *"I have been burgled. I don't like that. What needs to be done now?"*

Living in denial and wishing that the past or present moment was somehow different is a recipe for inaction and inner turmoil.

Life is short. Do we really want to spend significant portions of it bemoaning the fact that life is not the way we want it to be?

In fact, to live like that potentially doubles our levels of dissatisfaction. We are firstly frustrated that life is not different. Yet we then simply waste more time being frustrated when we could have gotten on and been productive. Like a vicious cycle, we end up being frustrated that we are frustrated.

We are like a child who wakes up and wants to play in the garden in the Sun. However, just as she opens the door, it begins to rain heavily and incessantly.

The day has not turned out the way she wanted. Yet, does it make the rest of the day more or less enjoyable by sulking all day? In that case, it is not so much the rain that ruined her day, but her failure to accept that it was raining.

What Acceptance is NOT

Acceptance does not mean resignation. By accepting your reality, you are not giving-in, and you are not surrendering. You are simply choosing your battles. You can either fight against your experience—and lose —or you can choose to acknowledge it, and thereby stop it from controlling your life.

Acceptance is not indifference. If you were caught in quicksand, you would not be wise to struggle against it. Neither should you be passively indifferent and just sink. Instead, you would most likely want to stop struggling, acknowledge the fact that you are in quicksand, lay back, and spread out. You neither fight nor ignore. You give yourself fully to the experience.

In the same way, acceptance is most certainly *not* approval or endorsement. This is a common concern of people who first encounter ideas like those found in this book. If you had been assaulted at some point in your life, by encouraging you to accept it, I am not at all suggesting that you should be glad it happened or be thankful in some way. Acceptance does not mean that.

Acceptance means recognising that the assault happened; acknowledging that it took place and moving on from that place of acceptance. The alternative is to deny the experience, smother it deep in your subconscious, and never reach a point where you are able to carry on with your life.

Acceptance is, in a very real sense, simply starting where you are.

What is Brief Acceptance?

We are using the term ‘brief' in two different ways:

Firstly, it refers to our bias toward 'brief therapy'—

understood as a commitment to resolving an issue in as short a time as possible.[3] In fact, many practitioners of brief therapy would suggest that prolonging sessions over an extended period of time can be dis-empowering and counter-productive.

Secondly, we are using the term 'brief' to invite consideration of—at least—*temporary* acceptance. Some people who are introduced to Brief Acceptance can initially struggle with the idea of accepting unpalatable situations. To be told that in order to move forward they merely need to accept reality as it is for now, can be accessible and empowering. It is often the first step toward freedom, productivity, and happiness.

Acceptance and Change

Imagine that you had a small pebble in your shoe. It was small enough to ignore most of the time, though it did make walking anywhere of any length quite painful.

What do you do if there is somewhere you want to go?

---

3 A popular example of brief therapy is Solution-Focused Brief Therapy, which focuses on a client's resources and employs a future-orientation.

- You could deny the pebble's existence and keep struggling on. (It is unclear how far you would get and how long you could take the pain for.)

- You could retrace your steps, attempting to find out when and why the pain started. (This would not make walking any more comfortable and would almost certainly be unnecessary.)

- You could acknowledge that the pebble is in your shoe, take it out, and keep walking. (It is only when you accept the reality of the pebble that you can do something about it and keep moving forward.)

So, Brief Acceptance does not say you can never do anything to improve your situation. If you *can* change something unpleasant, by all means, go ahead and change it. Brief Acceptance simply says that you need to accept something before you can do anything about it.

I am reminded of the Serenity Prayer, which almost perfectly encapsulates Brief Acceptance. You may be familiar with it:

> God, grant me the serenity to accept the things I cannot change,
>
> The courage to change the things I can,

And the wisdom to know the difference.

The prayer was composed by the North American theologian, Reinhold Niebuhr in the 1950's. However, we can see versions of it, or the thoughts contained within it, throughout time and in various cultures. There are hints of it in Epictetus in the first century CE:

> "Make the best use of what is in your power, and take the rest as it happens. Some things are up to us and some things are not up to us. Our opinions are up to us, and our impulses, desires, aversions-in short, whatever is our own doing. Our bodies are not up to us, nor are our possessions, our reputations, or our public offices, or, that is, whatever is not our own doing."

The 8th-century Indian Buddhist scholar Shantideva reasoned similarly:

> If there's a remedy when trouble strikes,
>
> What reason is there for dejection?
>
> And if there is no help for it,
>
> What use is there in being glum?

Finally, the Jewish philosopher Solomon ibn Gabirol wrote, in the 11th century:

> 'And they said: At the head of all understanding – is realizing what is and what cannot be, and the consoling of what is not in our power to change.'

You do not need to believe in God—or any particular spirituality—to find the Serenity Prayer inspirational.[4] After all, it seems to capture something at the heart of many schools of wisdom.

All you really need to do is start putting it into practice. After all, if Margaret can do it—after 30 years of struggle—you can too!

***

Margaret worked with me for 4 sessions. We explored some of the ideas of Brief Acceptance. She had an epiphany one afternoon that holding onto David and refusing to accept that he had gone had not brought him back. He was still dead, and Margaret, in her words, "may as well have been too."

---

4 I think of 'God' as our highest values, or that which we hold in most regard. For some people, this will be a supreme being of some kind, but that is not necessary for appreciating the words of the Prayer.

I did far more listening than talking in those 4 sessions. I merely dropped in a few ideas and left some hints as to possible ways forward. Margaret did all of the hard work herself. She is the one who articulated that by not accepting her husband's death, all she had done was re-experience him dying day after day for 30 years.

In our 4th session, Margaret said that she was feeling lighter than she had in years. Speaking of acceptance, she marvelled that something so simple could be "almost magical." Margaret said she had been practising acceptance and was now ready to let David go. She asked me to refer her onto a Grief Counsellor, which I did with pleasure.

A few years later, I ran into Margaret's daughter in the supermarket. (She was the one who had driven Margaret to and from our sessions.) She informed me that Margaret had passed away at the grand age of 104 and that she died exactly as she had lived her last couple of years—peacefully.

***

Focusing on Life, not Problems

It will be clear by now that the ultimate goal of Brief Acceptance is not symptom removal. This places it in stark contrast to most Western Psychotherapy.

For example, if you were to work with a Brief Acceptance Therapist due to constant and extreme anxiety, they may not even ask you what you are anxious about. Instead, they are more likely to ask what you would be doing in life if anxiety were not a problem. Or, even, "what do you want to be doing in your life right now?"

The ultimate goal of Brief Acceptance in such a situation is not the removal of anxiety. Instead, it is aimed at helping you to live a life you value, regardless of the presence or absence of any anxiety.

It may not come as a surprise to learn that if you do go on to live the life you value, with or without anxiety, you will often find the anxiety dissolving of its own accord at some point. This is not your primary intention, but it is a common and pleasant side-effect.

The real goal and focus of Brief Acceptance is to empower you to live the life you aim to. The removal of symptoms may or may not occur, but it does not really matter. If they no longer hinder your ability to live life as you choose to, they now have no power over you.

This focus on living your life is what we turn to in the next chapter.

CHAPTER THREE

The Life you Value

What are you all about? What gets you going? What stirs you, or inspires you, or sticks a rocket up your backside and sends you in to space?

Many of us can find these sorts of questions difficult to answer. After all, we might not spend much time really thinking about them, or their relevance. However, as we will see in this chapter, living in accordance with your values is a deeply satisfying and natural way to live.

If you are the kind of person who has not given this

much thought, you might consider asking one of your friends to assist you. Here are some questions for them to consider:

> "If someone asked you what my passion was, what would you say?"
>
> "Guess – if I won the Lottery, what would I spend it on?"
>
> "If someone asked you what I was 'all about,' what would you say?"
>
> "Imagine that my life goes just the way I want it to, what do you think would be written on my epitaph?"

A Values-Based Life

As we have already seen, the goal of Brief Acceptance is not for you to have a symptom-free life. It is for you to live a fulfilling life. And that means living a life that has purpose and meaning. And *that* means living life in accordance with your values.

So, what do we mean by values? What are they? What are they not? Why are they important? And how do you discover yours if you have never taken the time to figure them out?

Our values influence how we make decisions and effectively run our lives. Values can be instilled in us or we can choose to adopt them. Our values can change. Our values guide how we choose to focus our energy and time. The important thing to know is that when we have strong and positive values, they will be integral to our achieving what we want in life.

Values are how you see the world, what you see as important. Values are the direction your life is taking.

We never "accomplish" a value, they are not goals that we can complete in that sense. Rather, values are like a compass—they help us make choices based on the direction in which we want our lives to go.

Your Life After Death

An effective way to think about your values is to consider your funeral. I do not mean to be morbid here. We are not talking about facing your death. If anything, we are looking at facing your *life*, and diving straight in.

It is interesting to me that when people speak about a departed loved-one at a funeral, they will very rarely talk about their large house, their luxury yacht, their various cars, or any other possessions they had. (Which is strange, considering that TV and movies would have us think that everyone would be thinking about the reading of the Will and what they are to gain from this tragic death!) Instead, people will take the time to share stories, jokes, and reflections on how someone lived and the things they did.

And, almost without fail, those stories about the things that were done are told as an example of the kind of person that has just passed away.

So, let's imagine for a moment that you have lived a full and meaningful life. It has truly been a life well lived. As you look back on the life you have lived, you can allow yourself to feel a sense of pride and appreciation that your life has meant something important.

I would like you now to imagine that you have passed-on from this life; yet, you are able to attend your own funeral in spirit. As this is your imagination, you do not need to stick to the rules of logic when you consider who might be in attendance. Your parents might be there, even at the age they are now, though you are older. Loved ones who have died might be there too. Your friends, your children, your partner(s), colleagues, loved ones, role-models, and inspirations—they are all there.

As often takes place at funerals, some people have prepared some words to deliver in memory of you. Imagine who you would want the first person to be to stand up to speak about what your well-lived life looked like.

This exercise is more effective if you imagine a specific person. It could be a person who has already died, or someone you have not ever met. However, it will be someone whose wisdom, insight, and opinions are important to you.

What would you want that person to say about what they feel you stood for in your life? How do they describe the things that drove you? What did they most admire about you? Imagine that person actually saying those things you'd most like them to say.

Now imagine that a second person stands up. Maybe it is one of your children, or a dear friend. What would you want that person to say about what you meant to them? As they reflect on your well-lived life, what things would you like them to say were an example and inspiration to them?

Finally, one last person stands up. Maybe this is one of your parents, or a partner, or maybe someone from your community. What would you want this person to talk about in their eulogy of what your life has meant. What would this person say in describing your fulfilling life? What sort of activities or behaviours would they mention as an example of how you lived your life?

***

The day that Andreas broke both of his legs in a skiing accident changed his life. Before that date, he had been a rising star in one of his country's top football teams. After the accident, it was as if his spark went out entirely.

The realisation that he would no longer go on to be the top footballer he had dreamed of being for so long was unthinkable to Andreas. He drowned-out that thought with alcohol, fast-food, and narcotics. He lost his fiancé, his job, and most of his friends.

Andreas spent years living like this. He put on a dangerous amount of weight and was unrecognisable —in both body and personality—to those who had known him previously. He finally sought help when he overhead his elderly mother telling someone that, "my boy lost more than his legs in that accident. I think he lost his soul."

The thought of his mother dying and taking that notion with her to the grave was too much for Andreas to ignore. Remarkably, he contacted a therapist that same day, and within a week was telling them that he could not shake the idea of being at his mum's funeral and hearing the words, "he lost his soul" over and over in his head.

The Therapist asked Andreas to consider his own funeral for a moment. He asked him to think about the sort of eulogies he would hope to hear, even imagining that his mother was there. What would he want her to say about her son?

They then considered Andreas' graveside. The therapist talked about how the epitaph that we see on people's gravestones often aims to capture that person's essence, or how they lived, in just a few words. He then asked Andreas what he would like his epitaph to say about how he lived.

Andreas thought for a long-time before answering. "I just want it to say, 'He lived.' That would be a good start, wouldn't it?"

***

Valued Living Questionnaire

The following exercise will help you to consider different aspects of your life, using ten different categories. If there are certain categories that you don't particularly value, you can simply move on to the next one. However, think about the following areas and the questions listed, as they may help you explore and clarify the things you hold important and meaningful.

It can be useful to consider *why* they matter to you and which you consider the most important.

1. Family relations

What sort of brother/sister, son/daughter, uncle/auntie do you want to be? What personal qualities would you like to bring to those relationships? What sort of relationships would you like to build? How would you want to interact with others if you were the ideal you in these relationships?

2. Marriage/couples/intimate relationships

What sort of intimate partner would you like to be? What personal qualities would you like to develop? What sort of relationship would you like to build? If you were the person you want to be, how would you interact with your partner?

3. Parenting

What sort of parent would you like to be? What sort of qualities do you want to have? What sort of relationships would you like to build with your children? How would you behave if you were the parent you want to be?

4. Friendships/social life

When you consider your friendships, what sort of qualities would you like to bring to those relationships? What sort of friendships would you like to build? If you could be the best friend possible, how would you behave toward your friends?

5. Career/employment

What do you value in the work you do? What would make it more meaningful? What kind of worker would you like to be? If you were the worker you would you like to be, what qualities would you like to bring to your work? What sort of work relations would you like to build?

6. Education/personal growth and development

What do you value about learning, education, training, or personal growth? Are there any new skills you would like to learn? Or any knowledge you would like to gain? What sort of student would you like to be?

7. Recreation/fun/leisure

What sorts of sports, hobbies or leisure activities do

you enjoy? How do you like to relax and unwind? What do you do for fun? What sorts of new activities would you like to do?

8. Spirituality

Whatever spirituality means to you, what is important to you in this area of life?

9. Citizenship/ environment/ community life

How would you like to contribute to your community or environment? For example, volunteering or recycling or supporting a group, charity, or political party? What sort of environments would you like to contribute towards at home and at work? What environments would you like to spend more time in?

10. Health/physical well-being

What values do you have concerning maintaining your physical well-being? How do you like to look after your self, with regard to sleep, diet, exercise, smoking, alcohol, etc.? Why is this important to you?

Once you have answered these questions, you will be well-equipped to proceed with the following exercise. This will help bring some further clarity regarding your values and how closely you are living in alignment with them.

Write out each of the ten domains listed. Then, under each one, you are free to write a line or two to summarise your specific values in that category. For example, underneath the category of 'Parenting,' you could possibly write down the value, 'To be a loving, attentive, fun parent.'

Then, on the left, write a number that reflects how important this value is to you on a scale of 0 to 10, where 0 is not important at all and 10 is extremely important.

Next, write a second number on the right that reflects how you feel you have lived this value in the last month.

Intimate Relationships

1-10 1-10

Parenting

1-10 1-10

Family relations

1-10 1-10

Social relations

1-10 1-10

Employment

1-10 1-10

Education and training

1-10 1-10

Recreation

1-10 1-10

Spirituality

1-10 1-10

Citizenship / community

1-10 1-10

Health

1-10 1-10

Look at the values that have relatively high importance scores (a score of 9 or 10), and also have relatively low consistency scores (6 or less). These would seem to be obvious problem areas, highlighting a domain of life that is important to you and that you would find satisfying and fulfilling if only you were paying more attention to it.

Alternatively, you might discover that things that you

always held as essential values to you are not actually that important. You can then use this assessment as an opportunity to discover or admit your current true values to yourself.

Setting Values-Based Goals

Once you've identified a value, a useful question to ask can be, "What's the smallest, simplest, easiest action you could take, in the next 24 hours that's consistent with that value?"

This simple question gives us an immediate goal. Many people—including many therapists, business leaders, and Life Coaches—feel that they need to have short-term, medium, and long-term goals as well. If you sense that such goals might support you to live in line with your values, the following exercises—developing out of the question above—might prove useful:

> Short-term goal(s): List some things you can do in the service of your values-based goal within the next few days and weeks.
>
> Medium-term goal(s): Reflect on specific actions you can take to move toward your values-based goal within the next few weeks and months.

> Long-term goal(s): Make a plan of what actions will move you closer to your values-based goal over the next few months and years.

An alternative approach, more in line with the eulogy exercise earlier, would be to imagine yourself in a year's time having effectively lived your life as you value. What sort of things might you have done?

Next, consider your life after five years of valued living. What notable things might you have done in that time?

Finally, imagine it is twenty years from now. Twenty years of living life in a valued direction. What significant markers might you have passed along the way?

If you do think it would be helpful for you to unpack specific goals like this, it is useful to remember the SMART acronym regarding goal setting:

> S = specific (Do not set a vague, fuzzy, or poorly defined goal like, 'I'll be a better parent.' Instead, be specific: 'I'll give my children my full attention when I pick them up from school.' In other words, specify what actions you will take.)
>
> M = meaningful (Make sure this goal is

aligned with your most important values.)

A = Achievable (Is this goal likely to be fulfilled?)

R = Relevant (Is this goal relevant to you and your chosen direction in life? Is it a suitable goal at this point in your life?)

T = Time-sensitive (Put a specific time-frame on the goal: specify the day, date, and time—as accurately as possible—when you will take the proposed actions.)

***

Despite what numerous business and personal development books may tell us, not everyone finds goal-setting to be a necessary or helpful aspect of valued living. Personally, I feel that the key thing to bear in mind here is that it is not really about achieving a specific goal at all. Instead, goals are seen as confirmation; markers along the way that we reach as we proceed in our valued direction.

***

Leo Babauta started a humble blog - Zen Habits - in 2004.[5]

It was a simple blog, focused on quick and easy hacks

5 www.zenhabits.com

to leading a productive life. Today, Zen Habits has over 200,000 subscribers and has twice been named one of the Top 25 blogs by Time Magazine.

'In the past, I'd set a goal or three for the year, and then sub-goals for each month. Then I'd figure out what action steps to take each week and each day, and try to focus my day on those steps.'

As you can see, Leo is a do-er. (His first book was entitled, 'Zen to Done.') However, Leo is also honest about his successes and failures. 'Sometimes you achieve the goal and then you feel amazing. But most of the time you don't achieve them and you blame it on yourself.'

Leo discovered that although goals can get you moving, they can also very easily lead to discouragement and a perpetual feeling of not achieving that which you aim for.

'Even when you do things exactly right, it's not ideal. Here's why: you are extremely limited in your actions. When you don't feel like doing something, you have to force yourself to do it. Your path is chosen, so you don't have room to explore new territory. You have to follow the plan, even when you're passionate about something else.'

Today, Leo lives mostly without goals, and he finds it

liberating. Despite what we are often told, this did not necessarily lead to inaction. Instead, Leo discovered that it resulted in him no longer limiting himself by goals.

When some of Leo's regular readers discovered his new approach, they were perplexed. They challenged him that this must lead to wasting time and being lazy. On the contrary, Leo writes:

'You find something you're passionate about and do it. Just because you don't have goals doesn't mean you do nothing... In the end, I usually end up achieving more than if I had goals, because I'm always doing something I'm excited about. But whether I achieve or not isn't the point at all: all that matters is that I'm doing what I love, always.'

***

Living on Purpose

It may surprise you to find a self-help book that implicitly downplays the importance of goal setting. After all, achievement of impressive goals is often lauded as the pinnacle of personal development, especially in the West.

However, the risk of an *over*-emphasis on goals is that reaching that specific target becomes your focus. That means we can lose sight of how we are living here and now, obsessing instead over a future accomplishment. If that future goal is not reached for any reason—which, given the ups and downs of life, is a very possible outcome—we might then berate ourselves, or feel perpetually discouraged. That's hardly a *Brief Acceptance* way to live!

Instead, why not ask yourself, "What needs to be done now?" Find an action that you can fulfil in a way that reflects your values and *do it*.

If we want to get specific about this, this is about something deeper than values and goals. What we are really talking about here is doing that which is at the *core* of who you are. Doing that which is important to you is one thing. Doing that which you *have* to do is something altogether different.

Your values might be *being a good parent*, or *being a kind person*, or *living an active life,* and so on. Yet, it can be useful to ask deeper questions than this. *Why* do you want to live an active life? Why is *being a good parent* of great importance to you? Strictly speaking, we are not merely asking about your values here.

We are asking about *you*.

Who are you?

What are you all about?

What drives you, beneath the goals and targets and values?

You might say 'being a good example to my children' gets you out of bed in the morning. Yet *why* does that value prove effective? Why does it work? What is so valuable to you about that value?

What makes you tick?

And what keeps you going?

This is all quite theoretical, and it could sound quite unhelpful. After all, I asked you to move on from values to specifying some goals. And now I'm asking you to get vague all over again. Yet, in reality, what I am asking you to do is to go deeper.

Why do you value these values?

Why are they important to you?

And what does it say about you that these are the things that motivate you?

The reason why this deeper and vaguer series of questions may be important is because you will not always be able to specify goals. If you are not yet sure about your values either, or they are in the process or changing, simply find something that needs to be done, do it, and find value in what you do. In other words, you do not necessarily need to discover that which is most meaningful to you before you do anything. Simply do something that needs to be done and find the meaning in it.

You will not always find it possible to unpack how one of your priorities leads to specific actions. Sometimes, every now and again, you will just find a fire deep within. It may be difficult to name this fire... or speculate as to how it will express itself in your daily life.

Yet, if you are fortunate, you will find yourself handling a fire that is growing and flourishing, deep at your very core.

What is that like?

Now, go and do something that feeds that fire!

CHAPTER FOUR

Be Here Now

It is something of a cliché for a self-help book to talk about 'being in the moment,' 'living in the present' and so on. However, there is a reason why such ideas come up so often. Actually, as we will see later, there are a number of reasons why books such as this emphasise again and again the benefits of being in the here and now.

One of the common tools offered as a means of living this way is mindfulness. Although even the sound of that word can immediately turn some people off, we are going to devote this chapter primarily to the subject of mindfulness, arguing that it is far more than a recent craze or fashionable pastime.

Don't worry, I am not going to be ask you to become some kind of Zen monk, or meditation master. However, I will be offering you some exercises to practice, as a means to learning to live in the here and now.

Mindfulness, as an end in itself, is not what we will be recommending here. Instead, we will be using mindfulness as a tool to assist you to live in the moment, experiencing and accepting life as you encounter it.

Why are we looking at Mindfulness?

Mindfulness is a key element in a number of methods that promote acceptance. Whether that is Dialectical Behaviour Therapy (DBT), Mindfulness-Based Cognitive Therapy (MBCT), Mindfulness-Based Stress Reduction (MBSR), Acceptance and Commitment Therapy (ACT) or – to a lesser degree – Morita Therapy, mindfulness is offered as a valuable tool to utilise as we progress with a life of purpose and acceptance.

Throughout this book, you will see that a number of the skills we seek to develop utilise mindfulness. It is offered as an alternative way to relate to and experience our inner world. Yet, that is done precisely so we can accept it and thereby engage with our present moment and proceed with living a valued life.

Mindfulness is therefore a useful means of developing your acceptance skills. Being in the present moment, or the "here and now," means that we are aware (or mindful) of what is happening at this very moment. We are not distracted by ruminations on the past or worries about the future. All of our attention is focused on the present moment.

If we are to lead lives of accepting our experience 'as it is,' then cultivating our ability to focus on the here and now is essential. After all, the here and now is all there really is. Every experience we have takes place in the here and now. The past is gone and the future does not yet exist. All of our experiences are present moment experiences. Any unpleasant emotions we feel – as a result of those experiences – take place in the here and now. Therefore, learning to accept and live with such emotions requires learning to live in the present moment.

Being present helps you to worry less and to jump off of that rumination cycle. It keeps you grounded and connected to yourself and everything around you. It may seem like 'being present' and mindfulness are merely trendy fads. However, it is actually an ancient way of life that has a great deal of good science behind it.

Being present and practising mindfulness not only makes us less anxious and happier. It can also help us deal with pain more effectively, reduce stress and – significantly for practitioners of Brief Acceptance – improve our ability to cope with unpleasant emotions.

What is Mindfulness?

It is fairly common for people to equate mindfulness with meditation. Yet, whilst meditation is one way to effectively practice mindfulness, there is more to it than that. (In fact, when I am working 1-2-1 with clients, I rarely use the word 'meditation,' as there is no way of predicting if someone is going to react positively or negatively to that word.)

A more useful definition might be that offered by Jon Kabat-Zinn, perhaps the one person most responsible for bringing mindfulness to the West. He is also credited as the person who stripped mindfulness of any overtly Buddhist elements, making it a thoroughly non-religious endeavour.

Kabat-Zinn learned about and studied mindfulness under several Buddhist teachers, including Thich Nhat Hanh. This gave him an Eastern foundation in mindfulness that he then integrated with Western science to eventually develop Mindfulness-Based Stress Reduction (MBSR). This integration with Western science was a crucial aspect in helping mindfulness gain widespread popularity in the West.

Kabat-Zinn uses the following definition of mindfulness:

> "The awareness that arises from paying attention, on purpose, in the present moment and non-judgmentally"

The elements contained in that concise definition include:

1. The awareness
2. that arises from paying attention
3. on purpose
4. in the present moment
5. non-judgmentally

Another definition used by Kabat-Zinn, in the context of MBSR is:

> "Mindfulness is about being fully awake in our lives. It is about perceiving the exquisite

vividness of each moment."

I cannot deny that I am particularly fond of that definition. It resonates with me and immediately inspires me to live that way. However, with both of the definitions offered, we can see that mindfulness may be less of an activity that we take part in (like praying or pilates) and more a state of being that we learn to adopt. Mindfulness 'meditation' is a common way to access that state, but it is not the only way, as we shall see.

Benefits of Mindfulness

As mindfulness has grown dramatically in the public awareness and interest, it is easy for it to be dismissed as a fad. (I recently over-heard someone describe mindfulness as, "one of those trendy Eastern things"!) However, not only does mindfulness practice stretch back for centuries – and can be seen in a variety of cultures – it is also backed-up today with an extensive amount of academic research.

The following are just a few examples of what the studies have shown. (If any kind of academic talk turns you off – and you are already convinced of the benefits of mindfulness – you can feel free to skip this section.)

1. Improved Working Memory

According to a study by Amishi Jha and colleagues in 2010, mindfulness has been linked to enhanced working memory capacity. Additionally, by comparing samples of military participants who practised mindfulness training for eight weeks with those who didn't, Jha found evidence to suggest that mindfulness training also helped protect against losses to working memory capacity.

2. Heightened Meta-cognitive Awareness[6]

In non-academic terms, this refers to being able to detach from own own feelings and mental processes – to step back and perceive them as transient, momentary occurrences rather than 'who we are.' We will see the significance of this in a later chapter.

Studies have also proposed that mindfulness can decrease patterns of negative thinking behaviour (Teasdale, 1999). It seems promising that mindfulness may then have a positive effect in helping to avoid relapses into depression (Teasdale, 1999).

3. Decreased Anxiety

MBSR has been studied in-depth in a significant number of randomized, controlled trials. These frequently support its claim to have an impact on

---

6 Metacognition can be described as thinking about your thinking.

alleviating anxiety.

Vøllestad and colleagues found that participants who completed a course of MBSR had a medium to large positive impact on their anxiety (Vøllestad et al., 2011).

Studies on social anxiety have demonstrated similar positive results. For example, Goldin and Gross (2010) found evidence to suggest that MBSR training with socially anxious patients helped to improve anxiety and depression symptoms, as well as self-esteem.

4. Reduced Emotional 'Reactivity'

This, in my opinion, is an important point. There is some evidence to support the role of mindfulness in reducing emotional 'reactivity.' (If we feel angry, stressed, or hurt, we may have a tendency to react – or even overreact – impulsively. We are in a state of fight-or-flight and tend to react emotionally. That overreaction is what is meant by emotional reactivity.)

In an experimental task conducted by Ortner (2007), participants with more experience practising mindfulness were better able to disengage emotionally, when shown emotionally upsetting pictures. This means that they were able to show greater focus on the task they had been set.

5. Enhanced Visual Attention Processing

Another study by Hodgins and Adair (2010) found that those who practised mindfulness performed better on tests of concentration, selective attention, and more.

These results echoed earlier findings that mindfulness training stimulates improvements in attention, awareness, and emotion (Treadway & Lazar, 2009).

6. Reduced Stress

Mindfulness training has frequently been linked to lower stress levels. One example comes from Bränström et al. (2010), who found cancer patients who took part in mindfulness training had significantly reduced self-reported stress than those who didn't. They also displayed greater positive states of mind and fewer post-traumatic avoidance symptoms, such as loss of interest in activities.

7. Managing Physical Pain

There is some research which suggests that mindfulness may have a beneficial role in managing pain. Kieszkowska-Grudny's (2016) review of the literature on this topic included numerous studies into how mindfulness may help to manage chronic pain and help patients improve their quality of life (e.g. Goldenberg et al., 1994; Vowles & McCracken, 2008; 2011).

This list is by no means exhaustive. We could have looked at the role of mindfulness in developing and utilising better coping strategies, helping people sleep better, practising self-compassion, *and* building resilience.

Hopefully, this provides enough inspiration to begin looking at how mindfulness can help us in our daily lives!

Getting Started

As you begin to practice mindfulness, it can be useful to make a distinction between formal and informal mindfulness. Neither is better than the other, though you may find that you will naturally have a preference for a particular one. We will provide a few examples of both below.

Formal mindfulness more closely resembles what people think of when they describe *mindfulness* meditation. This may involve specific postures and precise steps for you to go through.

Informal mindfulness refers to activities that you might carry on mindfully as you go about your day-to-day business. This could include taking a shower, eating an apple, going for a walk, reading a book and so on.

Many people view informal mindfulness as the pinnacle to aim for. They approach formal mindfulness as a series of training exercises to elevate them to the plane where they live every moment mindfully. Whilst there may be *some* truth to this (in that formal mindfulness can help us become more acquainted with living in the here and now), it is not particularly helpful to view either practice as superior to the other.

Furthermore, if we treat formal mindfulness as merely a class to graduate from, we will ironically prevent ourselves from being in the present – as we are so focused on rising above what we are doing and reaching a higher level.

The reality is that both formal and informal mindfulness have their place. We may more naturally veer towards one rather than the other, which is perfectly fine. However, many practitioners continue with both methods of mindfulness, finding value in both the formal and informal approaches

I am throwing a lot of information at you in this chapter. So, now is the time to get practical. Please believe me that simply reading about mindfulness will most likely have no effect whatsoever on you, or your thoughts and feelings. Therefore, I invite you to read each description and spend some time engaging in it. Who knows? You might just love it!

***

The Body Scan (formal)

If you were taking part in a traditional 8-week MBSR course, one of the formal tools for developing awareness you would encounter is the Body Scan Meditation.

This involves actually feeling each region of your body that you focus on, lingering there with your full attention right on it (or even in it). You think about inhaling and exhaling out of each region a few times and then let go of it as your attention moves on to the next region. As you scan your body in this way, you will find that with each region you let go of, the muscles in that region let go too, releasing much of the tension they have been holding. It helps if you can imagine that you are breathing-in energy, vitality, and relaxation with each inhalation, and that the tension in your body flows out on each exhalation.

Here is Kabat-Zinn's description of the Body Scan Meditation:

[Start by] lying on your back and moving your mind through the different regions of your body.

We start with the toes of the left foot and slowly move up the foot and leg, feeling the sensations as we go and directing the breath in to and out from the different regions. From the pelvis, we go to the toes of the right foot and move up the right leg back to the pelvis. From there, we move up through the torso, through the low back and abdomen, the upper back and chest, and the shoulders.

Then we go to the fingers of both hands and move up simultaneously in both arms, returning to the shoulders. Then we move through the neck and throat, and finally all the regions of the face, the back of the head, and the top of the head.

We wind-up breathing through an imaginary hole in the very top of the head, as if we were a whale with a blowhole. We let our breathing move through the entire body from one end to the other, as if it were flowing in through the top of the head and out through the toes, and then in through the toes and out through the top of the head.

By the time we have completed the body scan, it can feel as if the entire body has dropped away or has become transparent, as if its substance were in some way erased. It can feel as if there is nothing but breath flowing freely across all the boundaries of the body.

As we complete the body scan, we let ourselves dwell in silence and stillness, in an awareness that may have by this point gone beyond the body altogether. After a time, when we feel ready to, we return to our body, to a sense of it as a whole. We feel it as solid again. We move our hands and feet intentionally. We might also massage the face and rock a little from side to side before opening our eyes and returning to the activities of the day.

...In the stress clinic it is in the body scan that our patients first learn to keep their attention focused over an extended period of time. It is the first technique they use to develop concentration, calmness, and mindfulness. For many people it is the body scan that brings them to their first experience of well-being and timelessness in the meditation practice.

At the same time, practising the body scan cultivates moment-to-moment awareness. Each time the mind wanders, we bring it back to the part of the body that we were working with when it drifted off, just as we bring the

> mind back to the breath when it wanders in the sitting meditation.[7]

You can practice the body scan briefly, or for a longer period of time. You might do it first thing in the morning, or as you are lying in bed at night. You can also practice it sitting or even standing. There are countless ways to incorporate the body scan into your life.

Mindful Breathing (informal)

Breathing regularly serves as the basis for mindfulness exercises because your breath is always with you, anywhere you are, and it can be used as an anchor to the here and now.

All that's involved is being mindful as you breathe in and out. There's no need to analyse what is taking place, count, visualise something, or seek to adjust your breath in any way. Just breathe normally and naturally and be conscious of your inhaling and exhaling. There are a number of methods you can use to focus on your breath. You can be mindful of your breath in your nose, chest, belly, or even your entire body as it breathes in and out.

When dealing with stress and anxiety, it is sometimes

7 Kabat-Zinn, *Full Catastrophe Living*, pp. 98-101.

recommended to practice abdominal breathing – breathing from the belly, rather than the chest – as this can be very calming and seems to help ground us. One of the benefits of abdominal or belly breathing is that it helps moderate irregular breathing patterns, which often arise due to stress. Anxiety can lead to shallow, rapid, or sporadic breathing and even hyperventilation.

By practising abdominal breathing, you are helping the body return to a natural balance. So when anxiety arises, first acknowledge the feeling, then gently bring attention to the abdomen and practice mindful breathing.

(You can check if you are breathing from your abdomen, by placing your hand on your belly and feeling whether it expands as you inhale and contracts as you exhale. If it doesn't, turn your attention to breathing more deeply and feeling your belly expand and contract with your breath.)

Mindfully Eating a Raisin (formal)

At the beginning of most MBSR courses, they introduce the simple practice of eating a raisin mindfully. It turns out that it is a surprisingly effective way of demystifying the concept of meditation.

As you do this practice, put aside all distractions, turn off the phone, and focus direct, clear awareness on each aspect and each moment of the experience.

Place a few raisins in your hand. (If you don't have a raisin, any food will do.) It can help if you imagine that you have just come to Earth from a distant planet without such food. Trust me on that!

Now, with this food in hand, you can begin to explore it with all of your senses.

Focus on the raisins as if you've never seen anything like it before. Focus on *seeing* the raisins. Scan them, exploring every part of them, as if you've never seen such a thing before. Turn them around with your fingers and notice what colour(s) they are.

Notice the folds and where the surface reflects light or becomes darker.

Next, *explore the texture*, feeling any softness, hardness, coarseness, or smoothness.

While you're doing this, if thoughts arise such as "Why am I doing this weird exercise?" or "I hate things like this," then just see if you can acknowledge those thoughts, let them be, and then bring your awareness back to the raisins.

Take the raisins beneath your nose and carefully

notice the smell of them.

Bring the raisins to one ear, squeeze them, roll them around, and *hear if there is any sound* coming from them.

Begin to slowly take the raisins to your mouth, noticing how the arm knows exactly where to go and perhaps becoming aware of your mouth watering.

Gently place the raisins in your mouth, on your tongue, without biting them. Simply explore the sensations of the raisins in your mouth.

When you're ready, bite down on the raisins, noticing if they go to one side of your mouth, or the other. Also notice the *taste* they release.

Slowly chew the raisins. Be aware of the saliva in your mouth and how the raisins change in consistency as you continue to chew.

When you are ready to swallow, see if you can notice the sensations of swallowing the raisin(s), sensing it moving down to your throat and into your oesophagus on its way to your stomach.

Mindful Eating (informal)

It turns out that eating is a great focus for

mindfulness. After all, everyone has to eat, yet we often do so while distracted by something else, like reading, working, or watching television. As a result, people often don't really taste or even notice what they're eating.

You can extend the approach of the formal practice of eating a raisin to any eating experience, allowing you to practice informally anytime you like. Simply give the experience of eating your full, undivided attention and intentionally slow the process down. Try to be like a scientific researcher, observing the mind and body with curiosity and objectivity, and without judgment. Go ahead and practice this several times over the next week. You're likely to find that your enjoyment of eating increases, while perhaps eating less, as you tune in to what your body really wants and needs.

***

Back in her mid-twenties, Elisha's life felt out of control. In an effort to redress this, she went on a one-month retreat. Each time they sat down to eat, they were instructed to be aware of what they were eating, where it came from, and the people who prepared it and to be thankful for it and eat it mindfully. Since Elisha was somewhat resistant to being there in the first place, she dug her heels in and just continued eating as she always had. Often, her mind would be swimming with doubts, questioning her decision to even go on the retreat, thinking she had more important things to be doing, and worrying about whether she even fit-in there. Most of the time she would be halfway through the meal before she even really tasted the food.

One day, as another participant in the program was talking to her about the importance of being intentional and present in all the activities they do, Elisha immediately thought of the eating and asked him, "Doesn't it annoy you that they make such a big deal about eating here?" He gently smiled at her, brought out an orange from his knapsack, and said, "Treat this as an experiment. Take this orange and really think about where it came from, how it started from a seed in the ground, how real people cared for the tree to make it healthy and then plucked the fruit from that tree. Think about how this orange was carried from there by many different people before it came to me, and now I'm giving it to you. Now, take this orange and drink it in with all of your senses before even peeling it, much less tasting it. When you are ready to take a bite, chew it slightly slower than you normally would, and then come back to me and let me know how it was for you." And then he left.

As she sat alone, Elisha noticed some resistance arising but decided to try his experiment nonetheless. She reflected on all the effort it took for this little orange to get to her, including the fact that it was a gift from another participant. She noticed that she felt a twinge of appreciation and a smile formed on her face. She had to admit that she liked that. Elisha looked a little closer and noticed all the tiny indents in the skin. As she slowly peeled the orange, she noticed a mist of citrus spring into the air, as though the orange was rejoicing to be opened, which made her laugh, and then she smelled the strong aroma. She noticed the contrast between the vivid orange of the outside of the peel and the pale, whitish inside surface. Once the orange was peeled, Elisha brought it closer to her eyes and saw the smooth, veined texture of the outer membrane. As she broke apart one segment, she really looked at all of the tiny individual pieces of pulp, swollen with juice. When she finally put a piece of orange on her tongue, tingling sensations ran up her cheeks. All of her attention was on the taste of the orange, and as she began to chew, she felt a rush of sheer delight at the amazing taste of the orange. She had eaten many oranges in her life, but had never tasted an orange in that way. And then she noticed that the distress she had been feeling was gone, and that she felt calm and at ease.

***

Mindful Check-in (formal)

Now we'll introduce a 3-minute practice to give you another taste of mindfulness: the mindful check-in.

You might want to congratulate yourself for taking this time for mindfulness practice. Then, take a few moments to be still.

Begin by feeling into your body and mind and allowing any waves of thought, emotion, or physical sensation to just be.

There is no need to judge, analyse, or figure anything out. Just allow yourself to be in the here and now, amidst everything that is present in this moment.

Spend approximately three minutes checking in with yourself in this way.

As you come to the end of this mindful check-in, again congratulate yourself for doing this practice and directly contributing to your health and well-being.

The Eight Attitudes of Mindfulness

It may seem a little late to introduce this, yet MBSR talks of eight specific attitudes of Mindfulness. This is a very helpful list.

The practice of mindfulness is somewhat like cultivating a garden: it flourishes when certain conditions are present. In terms of mindfulness, these conditions include the following eight attitudes, which some would consider essential to mindfulness practice:

1. Beginner's mind

   This quality of awareness sees things as new and fresh, as if for the first time, with a sense of curiosity and an openness to learning.

2. Non-judgment

   This attitude involves intentionally cultivating impartial observation in regard to any experience. There is no labelling thoughts, or feelings as good or bad, right or wrong, but simply taking note of thoughts, feelings, or sensations in each moment.

3. Acknowledgement

   This attitude and quality of awareness validates and acknowledges things as they are.

4. Non-striving

   There is no grasping, aversion to change, or movement away from whatever arises in the moment. In other words, non-striving means not trying to get anywhere other than where you are.

5. Equanimity

   This attitude and quality of awareness involves balance and fosters wisdom. It allows a deep understanding of the nature of change and allows you to sit with change with greater insight and compassion.

6. Letting be

   You can simply let things be as they are, with no need to try to let go of whatever is present.

7. Self-reliance

   This attitude helps you see for yourself, from your own experience, what is true or untrue.

8. Self-compassion

   This quality of awareness cultivates love for yourself as you are, without self-blame or criticism.

Holding these qualities in mind will enrich and strengthen your practice. These attitudes are interdependent; each influences the others, and by cultivating one you enhance them all.

Five-Minute Mindful Breathing (formal)

Now that you're familiar with some of the important foundations of mindfulness, you're ready to continue practising mindful breathing.

Do this practice in a relaxing environment, free from distractions. You can do it either lying down or sitting up, but if you lie down and find yourself falling asleep, try a more upright posture. Bring your full, undivided attention to this practice.

(You can practice anytime throughout the day, combining this practice with the mindful check-in, if you like.)

Take a few moments to be still.

Bring your awareness to your breath wherever you feel it most prominently in your body. That might be at the nose, neck, chest, belly, or somewhere else. As you inhale normally and naturally, be aware of breathing in, and as you exhale, be aware of breathing out. Simply maintain this awareness of the breath, breathing in and breathing out.

There is no need to visualize, count, or figure out the breath; just be mindful of breathing in and out. Without judgment, just watch the breath ebb and flow like waves in the sea. There's no place to go and nothing else to do, just be in the here and now, noticing the breath—just living life one inhalation and one exhalation at a time.

As you breathe in and out, be mindful of the breath rising on the inhalation and falling on the exhalation. Just riding the waves of the breath, moment by moment, breathing in and breathing out.

From time to time, attention may wander from the breath. When you notice this, simply acknowledge where you went and then gently bring your attention back to the breath.

Breathing normally and naturally, without manipulating the breath in any way, just be aware of the breath as it comes and goes.

As you come to the end of your five minutes, you can congratulate yourself for taking the time to practice mindfulness, recognising that this is a valuable act of self-compassion.

Mindful Exercising (informal)

In everyday life there are so many ways to move the body with mindful awareness. You can choose from stretching, running, yoga, tai chi, swimming, scuba diving, ice-skating, hang gliding, cycling, rowing, skiing, tennis, gymnastics, snowboarding, canoeing, skateboarding, walking, Pilates, dancing, football, table tennis, badminton, hockey, hiking, or working out at the gym or at home.

There are hundreds of ways to move and stay healthy. I would encourage you to mindfully practice any form of movement throughout the week.

15-min Breathing Exercise (formal)

This practice, a fifteen-minute version of the mindful breathing practice above, will support you in bringing yourself back to the present moment with greater awareness.

Remember that at any point you can use the breath as an anchor to come back to the present moment. Simply focus attention solely upon your breath. Don't try to control it. Just breathe normally and naturally, feeling it in the nose, belly, or wherever you feel it most prominently, being mindful of the breath rising as you inhale and falling as you exhale. Do this practice in a relaxing environment without distractions.

1. Assume a comfortable position, either lying on your back or sitting. If you are sitting, it can help if you keep the spine straight and let your shoulders drop.

2. Close your eyes, if you are comfortable doing so.

3. Now, bring all of your attention to your stomach. Notice it rise or expand gently as you breathe in and fall or recede as you breathe out.

4. Keep the focus on your breathing, being present with each inhalation for its full duration and with each exhalation for its full duration, as if you were riding the waves of your own breathing.

5. Every time you notice that your mind has wandered off, notice what it was that took you away and then gently bring your attention back to your belly and the feeling of the breath coming in and out.

6. Practice this exercise for fifteen minutes every day, for one week and see how it feels to incorporate a disciplined meditation practice into your life. Be aware of how it feels to spend some time each day just being with your breath without having to do anything.

Bringing the 8 Attitudes into Your Life (informal)

Try bringing the eight attitudes of mindfulness – beginner's mind, non-judgment, acknowledgement, non-striving, equanimity, letting be, self-reliance, and self-compassion – to yourself, other people, and the activities you do.

For example, if you're cooking, you can practice doing

it as if for the first time. Approaching the task with beginner's mind, feel the textures and experience the aromas as you cut onions, carrots, and greens, without any judgments about yourself, the food, or your cooking. Acknowledge your self-reliance—that you can care for yourself and others by cooking this meal.

If this is initially difficult for you, view it as an opportunity to practice self-compassion and be aware that you're giving it your best effort. Don't judge yourself if it doesn't all go the way you want it to go.

Notice how your body and mind feel when these attitudes are present, and how your mind and body feel when they aren't.

Try bringing this practice into other areas of your everyday life and see what happens to your relationship with yourself, others, and the world.

Weaving Mindfulness Throughout Your Day (informal)

By choosing to become mindful throughout the day, you can bring greater focus and appreciation to whatever situation you find yourself in. You'll also feel more calm and at peace. As you continue to grow in mindfulness, you'll see the potential for informal practice in any situation. If you need some help getting started, here are some suggestions for informal ways to weave mindfulness into your day:

- As you open your eyes in the morning, instead of jumping out of bed, take a few moments to do a mindful check-in. By starting the day with present moment awareness, you'll set the stage for a greater sense of calm and equanimity during challenging moments throughout your day.

- As you bathe, notice if your mind is already thinking, planning, and rehearsing for the day ahead. When you become aware of this, gently bring your mind back to the moment: being in the shower, smelling the soap, feeling the sensation of the water on your body, listening to the sound of it hitting the floor.

- If you live with others, try taking a few moments to listen and connect with them mindfully before you head out for the day.

- As you approach your car, walk more slowly, check in with your body, and notice any tension. Try to soften it before you begin your drive.

- When you drive, find opportunities to try driving a little slower. Use red lights as a reminder to notice your breathing.

- Walking is something we definitely tend to do on autopilot. As you walk to your office or to run errands, walk differently. For example, you might walk more slowly, or you could breathe in for three steps, then breathe out for three steps. Notice the sensations of walking—in your feet and throughout your body.

- If possible, maybe once a week, have a meal by yourself in silence, eating slightly slower than you usually do and tuning-in to flavours and textures as you eat.

- Throughout the day, do mindful check-ins from time to time. You can schedule them on your calendar, or you can link them to certain activities, such as prior to checking your email or before you drive home.

- It's counterproductive to rush home to relax, so try driving home mindfully and slightly slower. Feel your hands on the steering wheel, and mindfully take in each moment. You could turn off the radio and reflect on what you did that day. What was positive, and what would you do differently next time?

- When you get home, do a mindful check-in

> before you walk through the door, noticing if your body is tense. If it is, try to soften those muscles by breathing into them with awareness, just letting them be, and letting tension leave your body as you exhale.

As you begin to integrate informal practice into your daily life, take some time to reflect on your experiences. What did you do? What did you notice about yourself before and after the practice? How did you act or react to others? What are you learning from your mindfulness practice?

Floating Thoughts

Something that you will almost certainly experience as you begin practising mindfulness is a wandering mind. This is nothing to be concerned about. Even expert meditators can encounter this from time to time. In fact, the only difference between the experts and beginners is that the more experienced meditators will have learned to accept their wandering thoughts and let them be.

If you find your mind wandering off whilst you are practising mindfulness, it is important not to judge yourself – or your mind. You are not failing if your mind drifts off. Neither is your mind defective or unsuited to mindfulness. At such times, all you need to do is patiently notice and acknowledge the mind wandering – let it be – and then gently allow your focus to return to the breath.

In a rather ironic twist, a wandering mind can even be a good thing. Just think, if you were not being mindful, you would not have noticed that your mind had drifted off somewhere. As it is, we could almost say that the moment you realize you are not here and now, you have become present.

So, when you notice your mind wandering, appreciate it for helping you to be truly aware and gently bring it back. It has been said that even if you do nothing but gently bring your mind back every time it wandered, that would be time well-spent.[8]

Some people find it helpful to think of their thoughts as leaves on a river. You may be focusing on a lilly pad, but those thoughts keep on coming. Simply, let them be. Left to their own devices, they will soon float on by. They will only become a problem if you fight to stop them flowing down the river, or if you become fixated on one particular leaf. (If there is one thought that seems to keep cropping-up, rather than getting frustrated or fighting it, it can be helpful to thank the thought and then write it down. Then return to your mindfulness.)

8 Levey and Levey 2009, 64.

Finally...

We should note that if you were to take a MBSR class in person, you would discover that they rely on two main tools – mindfulness and yoga. I have not emphasised yoga in this chapter, as I am not sufficiently experienced to do the topic justice.

As you become more experienced with mindfulness, you may find that you are eager to incorporate more physical activities into your mindfulness practice. If so, you might want to consider learning to do any of the following mindfully: yoga, dancing, pilates, swimming, tai chi and running.

Some mindfulness courses will explain the primary purpose of each exercise. For example, "this body scan is great for awareness; the breathing exercises teach focus," and so on. However, I have intentionally avoiding doing so, as I believe that the purpose of each exercise can only be discovered through completing it.

The key is not which type of mindfulness exercise you do, or how long you do it for, or even where you do it. The key is to just start doing it. And then do it the next day and the day after that.

For this reason, we recommend that you set aside time every day for formal practice (anywhere from 5 to 45 minutes). Then, over time, you will find yourself more naturally living – and doing all that you do – in a mindful way.

All of the studies show one thing in common. That is, to reap the benefits, you need to find a way of practising mindfulness that works for you – and stick with it.

To gain a fuller understanding of Mindfulness-Based Stress Reduction, I would enthusiastically invite you to read Jon Kabat-Zinn's landmark book on the topic, *Full Catastrophe Living: Using the Wisdom of Your Body and Mind to Face Stress, Pain, and Illness.*

CHAPTER FIVE

Pay Attention!

'Life is Attention.' (Shoma Morita)

Morita Therapy is a Japanese psychotherapy, informed – in part – by Zen Buddhist principles. It adopts a holistic approach, aiming to improve everyday functioning rather than targeting specific symptoms.

Despite the fact that this book might be seen as focused on a mental or emotional state – acceptance – it is actually thoroughly action-based, drawing heavily upon Morita Therapy and similar approaches. Our goal, after all, is to show you how acceptance can empower you to *live the life you love.* Acceptance, in and of itself, is not the goal.

According to Morita Therapy, there is no right or wrong, or good or bad emotion. Emotion simply is. The only thing that is problematic about that is how we respond to the emotion and how much attention we give it.

Morita Therapy

I hope you will bear with me as I share a little bit about Morita Therapy and what attracted me to it. You will no doubt quickly see that it is *highly* relevant to our quest for brief acceptance.

Shoma Morita developed his therapy in Japan around 1920. Initially it was developed to help a condition that the Japanese called, *Shinkeishitsu.* Roughly speaking, this refers to a neurotic or anxious trait. We might think of it as a disabling anxiety disorder, accompanied by low mood.

Over time, Morita therapy was expanded to assist with a wide range of issues. However, it was originally focused solely on *Shinkeishitsu* – and that is the reason why it caught my attention.

Some of the common features found in someone with

Shinkeishitsu include:

- Anxiety
- Introspection
- Obsessiveness
- Perfectionism
- Self-consciousness
- Social withdrawal
- Over-sensitivity
- Hypochondria
- Mental and physical fatigue

Roughly 80% of the clients I work with are on the autistic spectrum. Almost all of them display more than one of the traits seen in that list. Yet, the more I worked with Morita therapy, the more I saw that *Shinkeishitsu* was not so much a condition or diagnosis, but simply characteristics that some people display at some times.

With this new understanding, it was easy to see that we all have *Shinkeishitsu* moments from time to time.

We can all obsess over mistakes we have made in the past. We can all, at times, be a little too self-conscious, introspective or anxious. And who among us has not experienced moments of flat-out mental or physical exhaustion?

So, I now think of *Shinkeishitsu* as less of a personality trait (though it may be more prevalent in some people) and more as an aspect of the human condition. Therefore, Morita therapy can be helpful, in some way, for all of us.

We will unpack various aspects of Morita therapy in this chapter and others to follow. However, for now, at the risk of gross oversimplification, we can summarise Morita's ideas with 3 over-arching points:

1. Accept your feelings

2. Follow your purpose

3. Do what needs to be done

Turning Our Attention Outward

Earlier this year, my 3 daughters and I went to visit a popular Country Park in our county. Unbeknownst to us, there had been some heavy snowfall in the Park and its surrounding areas. (We are so unused to snow in the UK these days, that we are never fully prepared for it. It doesn't help that we could literally encounter snow any time between November and May!)

It was a park we had visited numerous times before, enjoying the hills and valleys and apparently pre-historic surroundings. As we arrived at the park, struggling to park the car, it became obvious just how icy the conditions were.

We went for a bit of a hike, as we often did and found ourselves needing to traverse up and down some fairly icy hills. I can still vividly recall the intense attention I paid to every step, avoiding any icy slips and searching for solid ground.

For all I knew, at that exact moment, eagles could have been flying just above us, or there might have been a double rainbow, or a collection of sublime clouds and silver-linings. The point is, at that moment in time, I was solely and completely focused on where I placed my next step.

That was, of course, a perfectly natural response to ensure I acted safely, in line with my current environment.

Eventually – and much to my relief – we reached a point of flat and dry land. Almost without trying, I now found my attention turning to the wonders of nature around me. I noticed the soon-to-be setting Sun. I paid attention to the bubbling clouds on the horizon. I heard the birds singing and marvelled at the deadly Jurassic drop that surrounded us.

That second stage of our walk was far more enjoyable for me, more engaged in the world around us, more natural and more fulfilling.

Now, imagine that our walk carried on for another mile or more. After some time – especially because I am carrying a few more extra pounds than I could be – I might have noticed a twinge in my back and all of a sudden my attention would be self-focused once again. That is not necessarily right or wrong. However, it does ensure that I take my attention off of all of the natural beauty around me.

Morita believed that the flow of awareness in a person suffering from aspects of *Shinkeishitsu* was blocked and turned inward, away from the circumstances in which the individual actually found themselves. Thus the person's attention was solely focused on internal events (thoughts and feelings) rather than their external reality.

'Dreams seem real' Morita wrote, 'because no attention is focused on the external environment during sleep, and one's consciousness is extremely narrowed.'[9] We might say that the same thing happens

9 Morita, Shoma (1928/1974). *Morita therapy and the true nature of anxiety-based disorders (Shinkeishitsu), p.122.*

when we are too focused on our problematic thoughts and feelings. It sometimes seems as if we become entranced, fixated on the unpleasant feelings we are trying to avoid.

If we use anxiety as an example – a common characteristic of *Shinkeishitsu* that we all experience from time to time – we can find that the more we fight the anxiety, or struggle to avoid it, the more it increases, often accompanied by self-criticism, frustration and a diminishing of hope.

It is as if we get so caught-up in an eternal tug of war with our feelings, fearing that they will win, that we do not even consider the possibility that we could just let go of the rope, turn our attention outwards and get on with life.

As David Reynolds writes:

> 'Focus your attention on your feelings a lot and you end up miserable. Think of the people you know with the most satisfying, enviable lives. Do they ruminate about their emotions all day long? My guess is that they don't. Now consider the people you know who appear to be most miserable. Do they spend long periods of time dwelling on their feelings? I'll bet they do.'[10]

---

10 David K. Reynolds, *A Handbook for Constructive Living*. P. 4.

***

A colleague of mine, John, spends much of his time mentoring other therapists in using Solution-focused Brief Therapy. They soon discover an interesting and relevant point. This is a finding that John himself has seen previously and one that has been repeated by therapists across the globe.

John's students discovered that if they began a session by asking the kind of questions they would ask when using other models of therapy – such as, "So, what brings you here?" or, worse, "What seems to be the problem?" – it could be difficult to move on from that.

"It's as if the client would get themselves caught in some kind of loop. They appear to enter a 'problem trance' and very often the resulting conversation would contain lots of 'yeah, buts,' as they kept trying to return to their problem."

However, if the student therapists began the session by asking something like, "So, what is your best hope in coming here today?" or, "When you leave today, what will you need to have happened to ensure that it has been a beneficial use of your time?" there was a tangible difference in the air.

"It's like the client's attention is now on the positive possibilities before them, rather than finding

themselves stuck in the problem."

It is not that John is afraid of discussing a patient's 'presenting problem.' It is simply a recognition that if that is all you talk about, you might not make much progress. It is all too easy to submerge ourselves into unpleasant thoughts and feelings, without coming up for air.

***

What about Feelings?

Am I suggesting that internal feelings and emotions – pleasant or unpleasant – are irrelevant? Not at all!

In fact, as our earlier chapters have suggested, thoughts and feelings are there to be accepted. They are not to be ignored or avoided in any way. Brief Acceptance invites you to fully feel your feelings, accept them and then let them be.

After all, feelings and emotions are important. They may help us survive. They can be cues to take care of ourselves. Fear, for example, is a signal to avoid danger. Sadness prompts us to slow down and take time to grieve a loss, or recover from failure. It would be foolish to dismiss such useful emotions.

However, it is equally unhelpful to fixate on our

feelings. When our attention is solely focused on thoughts and feelings – especially those we judge to be unpleasant – we can find ourselves obsessing over experiences we would rather not spend too much time on.

It turns out that focussing our attention on a feeling or thought serves to strengthen it and increase its intensity. Additionally, it will draw our focus away from the reality of the present moment, or the world around us. We will end up ignoring the call to action that may have been contained within the emotion, instead choosing to obsess or grapple – and thus hold onto – the very thing we find so unpalatable.

Of course, there are times when an inward focus is understandable. If my left leg was on fire, I am sure you would forgive me for being focused on that! Similarly, serious toothache could make it difficult for someone to focus on anything other than their personal experience.

However, even with the examples we have chosen, it is not difficult to see that an outward-action focus is still possible. For example, your leg is on fire. That sounds awful. What are you going to do about it? How will you get that leg walking again? Or do you merely want to complain about the pain?

Your toothache is unbearable. I have been there.

However, there is more to your life than this one experience. How will you engage with the dentistry in such a way as to facilitate your return to living in the here and now?

These sorts of questions accept and honour your experience – allowing it to drive you forward into action. The only other alternative is to obsess and stagnate, fixating all of your attention on the very thoughts and feelings you wish to avoid.

As thoughts and feelings simply come and go of their own volition, we are not responsible for them and should aim to be aware of them without judgment. Attempting to control our feelings through a direct act of will is like trying to control the weather. It is far more sensible to simply let them come and go – and get on with whatever you had to do.[11]

For Morita, healing took place through an acceptance of emotions, thoughts and feelings, and the subsequent attention on the one area where control is actually possible – the realm of physical action.

***

The day before Jerry was due to fly out to speak at a

11 It is not that being aware of our internal experience is completely prohibited. The issue is that we can have a tendency to fixate on our thoughts and feelings, instead of allowing our minds to flow freely and to attend to that which is most pressing.

conference in the US, he went to his doctor about the anxiety that would boil-up inside him at the very thought of getting on the plane. Jerry's doctor explained that fear of flying was extremely common and nothing to be embarrassed about.

When Jerry took the prescription for diazepam to the Pharmacy, they asked him what it was for. "Fear of flying," he replied.

On the day of the flight, Jerry was jittery and doing everything he could to keep himself busy and distracted. As he reached the air-port, Jerry could think of nothing but the growing feelings of anxiety and nausea at the pit of his stomach.

Jerry boarded the plane, almost physically shaking. As he sat in his chair, he waited for the dreaded take-off and the predictable burst of panic inside him.

When the plane eventually elevated at quite an angle, Jerry felt what he expected to feel, confirming that he was responding precisely how someone with a fear of flying would.

There were occasional moments of respite. Jerry briefly got caught up in a film that was playing. Or he would think about the talk he was due to give, running through the main points in his mind. At those times, Jerry gave no attention to the fear and was therefore completely unaware of it, until he went looking for it once again.

He spent the majority of the flight acting and feeling the way he believed someone with a fear of flying would.

On the return flight, Jerry was sat next to someone far more fearful than he had been. He would call the stewards for reassurance with every moment of turbulence. He kept asking Jerry if everything seemed okay with the plane and generally relied on Jerry to keep himself from a continuous stream of panic attacks.

Jerry paid no attention to his own fear on that flight. He was so busy helping his neighbour that he did not give his fear a second thought. It was almost as if it was not there.

***

Feeling Our Feelings

One of my children, when she was younger, had an extremely high pain threshold. She also, rather ironically, had a strong aversion to blood.

I can remember numerous occasions when she might have been climbing trees with her siblings, or playing football, or chase. More often than not, she would end-up cutting herself on a branch, falling over, or hurting herself in some way.

Yet, as much as I try, I cannot recall a single occasion when she paused to acknowledge the pain, yelped out-loud, or even noticed the injury. Instead, she would rely on someone else to point out that she had cut herself. She would then cry-out at the sight of blood and panic over the unbearable pain.

Prior to noticing the blood, it would not be inaccurate to say that my daughter was not in pain. Similarly, it does not seem like an exaggeration to say that when he was supporting his fellow passenger, Jerry was no longer afraid of flying.

That which we focus our attention on grows. This is especially true of thoughts and feelings. Morita taught that all emotions eventually subside, unless they are reactivated. Keeping an inward focus on our feelings extends them beyond their natural life-time.

Instead, we can feel our feelings and then allow them to re-direct us outward towards meaningful actions. Such actions – and the actions we take to get there, as well as the actions which they lead to – are the stuff of life.

And it is life, not just our thoughts or feelings, that

deserves our attention.

CHAPTER SIX

Living Openly and Willingly

The Unwelcome Party Guest

Imagine for a moment that you are throwing a party – perhaps a barbecue.

It's a sunny summer afternoon and you have invited all of your friends over. They have all arrived and you are looking forward to a great time together.

You are all in the garden, enjoying the Sun. There is plenty of laughter that drowns out the sound of the music from your especially selected playlist.

Just then someone rings the doorbell, so you put your drink to one side, head to the front door and open it. Standing there greeting you is Brian, an incredibly annoying neighbour of yours. You really don't like him and certainly didn't invite him to the party. He is rude, obnoxious, selfish, always complaining and – to be honest – his hygiene could do with some work.

So, the second you see Brian standing there, you close the front door. But he keeps ringing the doorbell mercilessly, again and again and again and again...

Determined that there is no way he is getting into your party, you go and rejoin your friends and do your best to ignore the gate-crasher.

Yet, all the time that you're talking to your guests, you just keep hearing the ringing in the background. You do every thing you can to ignore it. You turn the music up, you try to get engrossed in various conversations, you employ numerous different strategies to try and ignore, avoid or drown-out that sound. But it just seems to get louder and louder.

Eventually, you go to the front door and you see if there is anything that you can do. Somehow, when you're letting another guest in, Brian manages to get his foot through the door and starts pushing the door. As you are not able to shut the door, you just decide to stand there and put your foot by the door to stop this unwelcome, annoying, rude and frustrating person from getting in.

You are pushing the door and trying to close it as much as possible. But Brian keeps pushing back. And somehow the stronger you push that door to try and keep this unwanted guest out, the more he seems to push back.

Meanwhile all your other friends are having a great time! They are outside in the garden having a barbecue – they're laughing and chatting with each other. But Brian is trying to get by the front door so you have to stand by the door and keep it as closed as possible.

You do this for a while and it is a generally effective way of keeping him out. After a while, he seems to stop pushing the door and has not rung the doorbell for a few minutes. Being on guard seems to have successfully kept Brian out. The only problem is that you are actually missing out on your own party! You know all the fun is happening outside and the whole point of the barbecue is to see your other friends. So, you make a decision – you are going to open the door to check if Brian is there and just see what happens.

You open the door and sure enough, in comes Brian rushing through the door and bumping into you in the process. And once he gets outside, he behaves exactly as you expected. He is rude, talks over the other guests, smelly, and just generally extremely annoying.

Some of the other guests seem a little shocked and when they look over to you, you convince yourself that they are wondering why you don't do something about this awful new guest.

It is difficult at first and you are not sure how to respond. However, you are determined to enjoy your party and strike up a conversation with a group of friends. After a while, you start to notice something unexpected. Some of your guests seem to quite like Brian. They are even laughing at his quirky sense of humour, which you had no idea he even possessed! You even suspect you could learn a thing or two from him, as you see him connect with others.

Although Brian was not someone you would have invited, when you finally let him in and started to interact with him in a nice way, you started to get some positive experiences. Sure, if you are honest, you would still have preferred it if he was not there. However, the great thing is, you were not stuck by your front door while everyone else was in the garden having a wonderful time.

You are able to notice Brian, but you also notice all of the other people too and enjoy their company. And as you started to think about him less, and no longer worried about whether he's there or not, or what he's up to, you actually start to have a really good time. And eventually, you almost forget that he is there because you are so engaged in the party and having such a blast.

Experiential Avoidance

This story serves to illustrate an idea that is core to Acceptance and Commitment Therapy (ACT). That is, the notion of *experiential avoidance*. This refers to our attempts to avoid unpleasant thoughts, feelings, physical sensations, and other internal experiences – even when doing so could create harm.

The unwanted guest, as you may have already worked-out, represents our unpleasant feelings, like stress or anxiety, sadness, depression or frustration. These experiences are the unwelcome guests that we have and usually we do everything within our power to make sure they don't get in. We try to keep the door closed, pushing them out the second they get in. We avoid them, deny them, fight with them, anything apart from letting them into our awareness. And that's where we see the in-built failing in experiential avoidance.

If we are determined to keep such unpleasant feelings out, we are only going to find ourselves stuck guarding the front door, rather than enjoying the party. Our determination to keep them out, merely binds us to them. We end up spending more time with them, compulsively paying attention to every thing they do.

Avoidance can often require super-human feats of strength and effort to keep it going. Such exhausting actions – which are almost always bound to fail – merely add to our unpleasant feelings and can leave us feeling trapped with the very sensations we are trying to avoid.

More than that, avoidance limits our attention, taking our focus off of the present and keeping us engaged in anticipatory anxiety. This is usually future-focused (worrying about what it will be like to encounter the unwanted guest), based on past negative experiences.

Experiential avoidance more often than not:

- takes our focus off of the present moment
- gets in the way of other important (valued) aspects of life
- increases the impact of unwanted feelings through over-attention on them

Why do we engage in Experiential Avoidance?

Given that these negative effects of avoidance may seem quite obvious, why is it that we engage in it so often and so easily? In short, it is a pessimistic act of self-protection.

If we get bitten by our neighbour's dog, we are likely to attempt to keep some distance from it in future. We may not even think about it. It just seems to make sense. It only really becomes a problem when our mind – which just loves to make patterns and associations – makes us wary of any and all dogs. Before we know it, we are no longer taking our children to the park at the weekend, due to the number of people who let their dogs run free.

So, with physical experiences, avoidance can be an effective strategy that makes some sense. It is at least understandable. It stops us from touching the stove when it is on, or ordering the over-ambitious curry which we always regret later. Yet, even then it can lead to more avoidance, as we focus so much attention on the issue and potentially magnify it in our minds.

With psychological experiences, things are different. Experiential avoidance usually increases the suffering it is meant to eliminate. The fact is, life involves unpleasant internal experiences and we simply cannot spend our lives hiding from them. The more we fight them, or avoid them, or run from them, the larger and more unpleasant they become in the process. You cannot out-run your unwanted guest.

***

Alan was on the verge of losing his job as a Bus driver. He had driven buses for just over 12 years and he was passionate about his job. (He and his partner even got married on an old-fashioned London bus!)

However, two years ago, Alan had been driving with his family in France. Before he knew what was happening, they were driving up an enormous bridge, that had his children shouting in delight, as if they were at an amusement park. Alan saw the cars in front of him slowing down and felt convinced they were going to end up stuck at the very top of the highest bridge he had ever seen.

That was the day that Alan would point to when he was asked where his phobia of driving over bridges began. From then on, he would plan his journeys to avoid going over bridges. Before too long, this even included normal dual carriageways that might cross over another road.

In a built-up city, this made Alan's job almost impossible. Any time he had to go over any kind of bridge, or even drive on a road that felt elevated to some degree, he would feel the rush of fear from France all over again. It made him a dangerous and unreliable driver, according to his employers.

Avoiding bridges had started as a way of not re-experiencing the panic Alan had encountered in France. In the blink of an eye, the amount of experiences he had to avoid grew exponentially – as did his fear of the fear.

***

What is the Alternative?

The alternative is so obvious that you may initially find it frustrating. However, bear with me.

Rather than taking part in experiential avoidance, we can seek to live our lives openly and willingly. This means quitting the practice of avoiding experiences because we're afraid of the unpleasant feelings that might come with them. We do not want to feel those feelings, we just stop letting them dictate the way we live our lives.

We are open to whatever life-experiences come our way, choosing to let our values direct our actions, not our inability to withstand discomfort. As we are committed to living a full and meaningful life, we are willing to experience unpleasant feelings in order to live the life we value. That does not mean that we enjoy spending time with our unwelcome guests. It simply means that we choose life – with all of its ups and downs – rather than retreating into a directionless existence of fear, avoidance, paranoia and suffering.

Once we are willing to face our emotional suffering, we can begin making choices based on passion, rather than aversion, values instead of fear. Whilst we may have previously focused all of our attention on protecting ourselves from unpleasant sensations, we can now become interested in doing what seems right or fun or meaningful or adventurous.

We dive into the party, instead of standing guarding the door.

Here is an interesting question to ask yourself.

> What might I do if I instantly stopped trying to avoid emotional pain?

Try to think of at least three answers. You might think of things you could experience, places you could go, things you might say, people you could spend time with...

***

Alan booked-in to see me. However, there was some delay and it was another 4 weeks before he was in my clinic.

"I feel a bit silly being here," he said, when we met. I asked why and he said that he had solved the problem by himself. However, he had still come to his appointment because he was interested in hypnosis and thought it could possibly cement the positive changes he had already made.

I congratulated Alan on solving the issue, suggesting that it is always more effective when clients find the solution for themselves. Then, my curiosity getting the better of me, I asked him how he had resolved things.

Alan said that as he thought about coming to see me, he worried that I might use some kind of exposure therapy with him. (That would mean, gradually introducing him into the situation he feared, progressively experiencing more and more over time.) Alan decided he could not face that and began typing an email to me, cancelling our session.

Then, before Alan had a chance to click, "SEND," he had a realisation. He was avoiding therapy because he thought it might involve experiencing a little bit of that which he feared. Additionally, he was hardly driving anywhere now, due to his fear of driving over bridges. Furthermore, he had never encountered another bridge like the one in France, before or after.

"And then I realised," Alan said, "that I was still

experiencing the fear. Avoiding that fear I had experienced in France simply resulted in me feeling that fear again and again in all sorts of otherwise unthreatening situations."

Alan told me that he actually laughed out-loud when he came to that realisation. He added that he was not willing to allow one experience with one bridge in France to dictate how he drove the rest of the time. "I'm not letting that steal my job, or my freedom," he said.

***

Being Open and Willing

When we are willing to feel unpleasant feelings, what often happens is that – predictably enough – we do sometimes feel bad. However, we find that we do so without the added stress of meaningless avoidance.

When we are open to accepting the totality of our experiences, the possibilities before us increase. So many more paths are available to us on the road of valued living. We will encounter emotional discomfort along the way. Yet, we will also discover that emotional pain ebbs and flows. Like the leaves on the river (in our mindfulness practice), unpleasant feelings – when left to themselves – come and go.

It turns out that the alternative to experiential avoidance is brief acceptance!

I am not suggesting that it is easy to open up to all of life's experiences. However, I am convinced that it is a far more satisfying way to live. When we learn to live alongside emotional pain – what Morita therapy calls 'co-existence with unpleasant feelings' - we learn to tolerate the lows with the highs, recognising that this is how life is designed to be.

Shoma Morita referred to our thoughts and feelings as "mental weather." They are things that happen to us, with which we can co-exist, but not directly control. If it is a sunny day, you cannot change that. You just have to find a way to live with it. If it is raining, it is raining. It just is. So, what are you going to do? You can't change the weather, but you can control how you act.

One of my favourite quotes from Morita is relevant here:

> "If it is raining and you have an umbrella, use it."

If not, what else are you going to do?

CHAPTER SEVEN

Skilfully Tolerating Distress

In this chapter we are going to focus on developing a series of skills that can assist you to tolerate negative emotions. These skills will be taken from an acceptance-based therapy that goes by the grandiose name of Dialectical Behaviour Therapy. We will refer to it via the more user-friendly "DBT."

One of the core practices behind most of the other elements of DBT is mindfulness. So, if you have been practising the exercises in chapter 4, you will already be ahead of the game. Mindfulness serves as a foundation for the other skills taught in DBT precisely because it helps people accept and tolerate the strong emotions they can feel when facing upsetting situations.

Distress Tolerance

We are going to spend the majority of this chapter exploring what are known as 'distress tolerance' skills. Distress tolerance skills are a natural evolution from mindfulness skills. They have to do with the ability to accept, in a non-judgmental fashion, both yourself and the current situation. Since this is a non-judgmental stance, this means that it is not one of approval or resignation. The goal is to become capable of calmly recognizing negative situations and their impact, rather than becoming overwhelmed or hiding from them. This allows us to make wise decisions about whether and how to take action.

Skill #1 : Self-Soothing with Your Five Senses

By focusing on your five senses, you're shifting your attention from the stressful situation to something entirely different. This helps you reconnect with your complete self and the world around you in a moment of crisis.

- Sight: Stimulate your eyes by seeing something. You

could go people-watching, or window-shopping. You might construct a fireplace or light a candle and lose yourself in the flame. You can go to a park and revel in the beauty of nature. Watch the sunrise or sunset.

• Hearing: Go outdoors and focus on the leaves rustling in a current of air, water flowing where it so desires, or the beeps and honks of traffic. Notice the windy hustle and bustle of the city.

• Taste: Eat your favourite meal or make a relaxing cup of tea or coffee. Chew a piece of gum or pop the bubble-gum in your mouth. Whatever you choose, focus on actually tasting the meals one item at a time.

• Touch: Pet your dog or cat. Sink into a comfy chair. Take a warm bath, or curl up in your favourite blanket.

• Smell: Burn some incense or a scented candle. Open a window. Take a bath with your favourite soaps, or afterwards splash on your favourite perfume or cologne.

Skill #2 : TIPP Skill

The TIPP Skill is unique because it relies on physiological principles. This is one of the most effective and quickest skills for reducing extreme emotion.

• T – Tip the Temperature: Put your face in a bowl of ice water or hold a zip-lock bag of ice to your face, eyes, cheeks and temples.

• I – Intense Exercise: Use all of that stored up physical energy that your emotions are creating and channel it into something like running, lifting weights, doing star jumps, or playing a physically demanding sport. Work up a good sweat.

• P – Paced Breathing: Slow your breathing down. Take big deep breathes in through your nose and exhale for even longer periods through your mouth. Focus. Try breathing in for five seconds and then breathe out for seven seconds. Repeat for as long as you feel necessary.

• P – Paired Muscle Relaxation: Whilst inhaling, tense the muscles in your body. Take note of how that tension feels. When you breathe out, let go of that tension and notice the change in your body. At first, try it just using the muscles in your legs or your arms. Then move onto other muscle groups.

Skill #3 : Cold Water

We can take the T from TIPP and make use of a great physiological response to use when we're in crisis. Hold your face under cold water for 15 to 30 seconds.

This seems to trigger a response in your brain that is sometimes referred to as the "dive response."

Essentially, your brain literally thinks you're diving underwater. To compensate and protect your body, your brain slows down your heart rate. Blood flow to your extremities slows down and blood is redirected to vital areas of your heart and brain.

This can be a very effective skill to use when you're experiencing extreme or very strong emotions. Find a safe, quiet place to try it for yourself.

Skill #4 : Paired Muscle Relaxation

This skill, originally encountered as a small part of the TIPP skill, is very similar to the Mindfulness body scan we described in chapter four. By practising mindful awareness of our body, we are able to connect our brains to present experiences more easily, which can lead to our brains being more accepting of reality.

If this will be the first time you have tried paired muscle relaxation, find a quiet, distraction-free setting and set aside ample time to fully explore its benefits. As you practice paired muscle relaxation more often, you might gradually venture to places with more outside stimuli to truly understand how you can use this skill in stressful environments.

Once you've found a good space, get your body into a comfortable position. It might also be helpful to loosen any tight fitting or restrictive clothing as well.

Now you're ready to get started:

• You will be working with most of the major muscle groups in your body, but for convenience we will make a systematic progression from your feet upwards. Here is the most popular sequence:

• Right foot

• Right lower leg and foot

• Entire right leg

• Left foot

• Left lower leg and foot

• Entire left leg

• Right hand

• Right forearm and hand

• Entire right arm

• Left hand

• Left forearm and hand

- Entire left arm
- Abdomen
- Chest
- Neck and shoulders
- Face

For each muscle group and body part, concentrate on tightening your muscles – focusing both on the sensation of tightening those muscles and how it affects surrounding areas.

Hold that tension as you inhale for about five seconds then release and breathe out.

As you release tension, slowly say "relax" in your mind.

Take note of the different sensations you encounter as you relax for about 10 to 15 seconds then move to the next body part or muscle group.

Once you've practised on each of the smaller, individual muscles or body parts, move on to tensing multiple medium-sized muscle groups together, then larger groups.

Next, try tensing your entire body all at once. When you tense your entire body, think of yourself as a stiff piece of steel. As you release that tension, think about being a rag doll and let your body droop.

After you're practised at full-body relaxation, practice it three to four times a day. You want to be able to quickly relax your body at a moment's notice.

With enough practice using the word "relax" paired with your muscle relaxation, you can eventually train yourself to relax your entire body by just saying the word "relax."

Practice helps the skill come more naturally to you when you need it.

Skill #5 : Radical Acceptance

The last group of Distress Tolerance skills is known as radical acceptance. As you might have guessed, these include some thoughts and exercises we have already introduced.

I have grouped aspects of these skills together in the following 10 steps:

- Observe that you are fighting against reality.

- Remind yourself that the unpleasant reality cannot be changed.

- Acknowledge that something led to this moment.

- Practice acceptance with not only your mind, but your body too. Be mindful of your breath and posture.

- List what your behaviour would look like if you did accept the facts, then act accordingly.

- Plan ahead with events that seem unacceptable and think about how you could appropriately cope.

- Remain mindful of physical sensations throughout your body such as tension or stress.

- Embrace feelings such as disappointment, sadness, or grief.

- Acknowledge that life is worth living even when there might be temporary pain.

- If you find yourself resisting, complete a pros and cons exercise to better understand the full impact of your choice.

Skill #6 : Radical Acceptance Coping Statements

Another way to practice radical acceptance when you are dealing with emotions, thoughts or a situation that you have a hard time accepting, is using *coping statements*.

These statements are designed to remind you that

there are some things you can not change. By accepting reality as it is, you can free yourself from the struggle of emotional tension, experiential avoidance and judging your thoughts.

In the list below I have provided you with examples of coping statements you can use. I would encourage you to consider which ones you like and then you could even write them down so that you have them ready to use at all times:

1. The present moment is the only one I have control over.
2. Fighting my emotions and thoughts only gives them more fuel to flourish and expand.
3. This moment is exactly as it has to be given the thousands of variables that have gone before it.
4. Fighting the past only blinds me to my present.
5. I cannot change what has happened in the past, but I can learn from it.
6. I accept this moment as it is.
7. Although my emotions are uncomfortable, I will get through it.
8. It's not helpful for me to fight the past.

9. This doesn't change my values, which are...

10. This is where I am right now. So, now what?

If you can think of other coping statements that suit your situation better, write them down and keep them somewhere handy. You don't have to limit yourself to the ones I have suggested.

CHAPTER EIGHT

Don't Believe Everything you Think

The title of this chapter may seem like a witty comment, or a joke to some people. However, it is offered as some of the most helpful advice you might receive in regards to living a life of acceptance.

As we learned from Shoma Morita, our thoughts are 'mental weather.' They come and they go. It is what we think about our thoughts – and how we relate to them – that is more significant than our thoughts themselves.

So, although when we have a thought, it might seem as if it is true – often by the very nature of the fact that we are thinking it – there is actually no reason that we are required to believe our own thoughts.[12] In fact, most of the exercises and techniques I will introduce in this chapter are designed to assist you to create some distance between you and your thoughts.

When we fail to maintain a sufficient distance between us and our thoughts, we can find ourselves tangled-up in our own thinking, ensnared by what might have been just a fleeting thought. In Acceptance and Commitment Therapy, they refer to this as *cognitive fusion*, or being fused to our thinking.

The first step in becoming untangled (or de-fused) is to notice our thoughts. This does not mean obsessively monitoring everything that passes through our mind. That would be no better than the entanglement we are seeking to release ourselves from! Instead, merely begin to notice when you are having a thought from time to time.

Rather than believing you are a loser, because that thought entered your head, with practice you will learn to be able to say, "I am having the thought that I am a loser." In fact, this is our first exercise.

---

12 Cf. Get Out of Your Mind and Into Your Life, p. 54.

Observing Your Thoughts

Steven Hayes refers to this as 'looking *at* your thoughts, rather than *from* them.'[13] The most basic way to begin practising this was seen in the last paragraph. Simply add, "I am having the thought that..." in front of any thought you notice.

So, for example, the following thoughts might have less of an impact when we add "I am having the thought that..." in front of them:

"I am a loser"

"I am too fat"

"Nobody here likes me"

"I never succeed at anything I do."

When we are totally entangled with these thoughts, there is no distance between the thought and our perception of what is real. That is, we believe the thoughts simply because we think them. However, noticing that we are having the thoughts often defuses them immediately:

"I am having the thought that I am a loser"

"I am having the thought that I am too fat"

---

13 Get Out of Your Mind and Into Your Life, pp. 65, 69-70.

"I am having the thought that nobody here likes me"

"I am having the thought that I never succeed at anything I do."

As you can see, we are no longer making a statement about reality, or vouching for our thoughts. We are simply stating that a particular thought is currently going through our minds.

You can even take this further and begin to notice what you are observing:

"I am noticing that I am having the thought that I am a loser."

With practice, you will sometimes find yourself doing this without even planning to. You will simply develop the skill of placing some distance between your thoughts, your understanding of what is real and yourself.

Mindfulness

We have already begun to create some distance between ourselves and our thoughts through aspects of practising mindfulness. I previously suggested that any distracting thoughts could be placed on a leaf that floats down the river. You can continue that very exercise when learning to become untangled from your thoughts.

Some people recommend imagining a slow-moving stream. Notice as much detail as you can – what does it look like? What does the water sound like? What smells are in the air? And so on. It can even help to imagine that you are sat beside the river as you are taking in all of this detail.

Then, whenever a thought appears in your head, you can see it as a leaf that drops onto the stream and is carried away down the river. Simply watch that thought come and go as a leaf dropping onto the stream.[14]

Lemon Lemon Lemon

This is a classic exercise from ACT that is usually referred to as the *Milk Milk Milk exercise*. However, I am especially keen on the variation used by some ACT therapists: *Lemon, Lemon, Lemon.*

Begin by simply saying the word, "Lemon."

As you do that, what images come to mind? Perhaps a

14 Steven Hayes makes the helpful note that if you think primarily in words, you can put the words of the thought onto the leaf. However, if you tend to think in pictures, you can put the thoughts onto the leaf as an image. See *Get Out of Your Mind and Into Your Life*, pp. 76-77.

personal memory of lemons pops up. You can go on to think of the colour, shape and size of a lemon.

What happens when you think about smelling a lemon? What do you notice?

Next, imagine placing the lemon on a chopping board and cutting it in half. Hear the sound of the knife cutting through the lemon and see the juices flow. Now, cut a wedge from one of the halves and hold it up to your mouth. How does it smell?

Now open your mouth and bite into the lemon. What happens now? What images come to your mind? Did you notice any new sensations in your body? Were you aware of your mouth salivating?

This simple exercise demonstrates both the power of language and imagination. Merely by saying the word "lemon" and then thinking about that lemon and all of the associated thoughts and feelings that brought up, you probably had a very real experience of biting into a lemon and reacting physically.

If thinking the word "lemon" – and investing in that thought – can effect our reality, just think what happens when we believe some of the negative words we tell ourselves!

The next stage in the *Lemon Lemon Lemon* exercise is to repeat the word "lemon" as fast as you can for 1 minute. Please don't just read those words. Actually do this.

"Lemon, lemon, lemon, lemon, lemon..." (Keep going, faster and faster for roughly 60 seconds.)

How was that? What did you notice? What happened to the word "lemon"?

Many people report that the word begins to feel like it is just a bundle of sounds. Or, you might have started laughing a little, especially as you increased in speed.

Perhaps the word stayed in tact, but lost much of its meaning and associations. It most likely did not have the same effect as when you thought of a lemon the first time.

I wonder what effect it would have if you went through this exercise with some of the thoughts you become entangled with.

What happens when you try this exercise with the following words:

"loser"

"fat"

"Nobody likes me"

"Never succeed."

Do you notice any difference to the effect the thought or word has on you? They might feel less 'real.' Or they might just sound like a jumbled pile of sounds. With practice, I am sure you will find that at the least this exercise helps to create some distance between the thought, what you think about that thought and your current experience of reality.

Mind-chatter exercises

We can expand on the Milk/Lemon exercise by continuing to play around with words. Think of a thought you have that almost always has an automatic effect on you, creating anxiety, despondency, or other feelings. It may be something like, "You'll never do this!", "They think you're stupid," or similar.

We are now going to experiment with your internal voice, or "mind-chatter," to see if it might make a difference to how entangled you can feel with your thoughts.[15]

Auditory Manipulation

Pay attention to a particular thought or statement you make to yourself. I'm talking about the specifics we do not normally even notice – like, where is the statement in your head? On the left, the right? Behind

15 This content originally appeared in *The Anxiety Guide*.

you or in front? (These questions will sound completely nonsensical until you actually do this!) Either way, change the location, e.g. swap sides, and see if this changes how you feel when you hear the statement.

Next, think about *how* you made those statements. Did you say them in your normal conversational voice, or was it said at a faster tempo? If your mind-chatter was faster than usual, go ahead and repeat it to yourself, about one-third slower than you usually say it.

Reduce the speed once again and repeat the statement. Pay attention to how that changes what you feel.

Then, once more, reduce the speed of what you say to yourself. And notice what is different.

Now, when you try to think of that occasion as you used to, what can you notice that is different?

Some people prefer to change more than the speed of the voice. I read about someone who changes the voice to that of Minnie Mouse, so I went ahead and changed my thought's voice to Bart Simpson. When I did that, no matter what the voice said, it was difficult to take it seriously!

If you struggle with historic things said to you, that perhaps still have an impact, making you feel anxious or worthless, try changing the voice into that of a precocious child or a sulky pre-teen. You may find that you no longer care as much about what they have to say.

Visual Manipulation

You can also imagine seeing the words of your thought spray-painted on a wall, as the train you are on passes by them. Or see them on a banner pulled by a blimp. Perhaps they will feel different when read, rather than heard? Again, you may want to experiment with spacing the letters out more, changing the size of the words, or moving them closer or further away from you.

For starters, begin to slow down the train, or blimp, spreading the words out as you do so. Begin to spread the words in such a way that you start to pay more attention to the space between the words, than the words themselves. Carry on to separate the letters as well, and again pay attention to the spaces, rather than to the letters.

What has happened to that thought now? Do you notice any changes in the effect it has on you? Does it now feel more like something you say in your head, rather than something you unquestionably believe?

***

Jess had vowed to herself that she would not bring her children up the way she had been brought up. Her parents were extremely strict and as a child Jess felt like she was always in the wrong.

When her daughter was born, Jess was delighted and more than a little terrified! She felt like the only thing she knew about raising a child was how not *to do it. So, she ensured that play and laughter and warmth and encouragement were a constant feature of life in her home.*

Predictably, Jess' parents did not approve of the way she raised her child. Jess had expected and was prepared for that. However, she was still taken aback to hear her mother say, "I can't say I'm surprised. I never expected you to be a good mother."

As much as she tried, Jess could not shake those words from her head. Over time, they morphed into the thought, "I am a lousy mother," which looped round and round Jess' head almost every waking moment.

When Jess found herself pregnant for the second time, she realised that she had lost all confidence in her parenting abilities. She also realised, for the first time, that she was no longer enjoying being a parent. She dreaded the thought of having two young children to look after, convinced that she would do so poorly.

Jess spoke to Abby, a Support Worker at her local

Children's Centre. Abby had found relief from much of her anxiety through reading my book The Anxiety Guide. *So, she shared some of the ideas with Jess, guiding her to manipulate the words that she kept repeating to herself – "I am a lousy mother." Jess found great delight in hearing that thought in the voice of Frank Spencer (from the BBC comedy,* Some Mothers Do 'Ave 'Em*) and told Abby that she would keep practising.*

The more she carried out the exercise, the more the thought began to seem funnier and funnier. After all, no one ever took Frank Spencer seriously and to hear him saying, "Oooh, I am a lousy mother!" made Jess smile.

A few weeks later, Jess popped into the Children's Centre and Abby asked how she was getting on. "It's amazing," said Jess, "I honestly find it difficult to remember why I let those words bother me. And I laughed at the idea that I ever let my mother – who was such a poor example – ever effect how I thought about myself as a parent."

Jess informed Abby that she had not got all of her confidence back, but she had at least reached a point where she felt like she could be a good mother. She signed-up for a parenting course at the Children's Centre, telling Abby that she knew that she had it within her to be a great parent. She now just wanted to brush up on her parenting skills and said that she looked forward to hearing her mother saying that she was a bad mother. "To hear that from her," she said, "would mean I was doing a great job!"

***

Do You Buy Into This thought?

As we have seen, there is a difference between having a thought and believing that thought. One effect of the defusion exercises you have practised in this chapter is to highlight that difference, allowing you to experience the distance between the thought and belief in the thought.

Continued practice with these exercises will not only help you to become de-tangled from specific thoughts. It will also help you to retrain the tendency you may have to automatically buy-in to each and every thought that pops into your head.

This notion of buying-in to a thought provides us with our final defusion exercise.

To start, notice a thought you are currently having. Then notice that you are noticing it. You might say something along the lines of:

"I notice that I am having the thought that I

> am a fraud."

We can now distinguish between having this thought and buying into it.

As you notice that you are having the thought that you are a fraud, what do you now want to do with that thought?

Carefully consider the thought. Observe it from a distance. Then inspect it from different angles, the way a jeweller may check the quality of a gemstone.

Then ask yourself if this is just a thought you are having, that can come and go, or is there a chance that it is a thought that you can choose to buy in to.

It can help to do this if you start by labelling your thoughts. These are not judgements, but descriptions of the thought, or its function. For example, "this is a critical thought." Or, "this is comparison." Alternatively, you might say something like, "I am having that old thought that I am a fraud."

Having labelled your thought, bringing it into the cold light of day and making it a concrete rather than abstract item, you can now ask yourself:

> "Do I want to buy the thought that I am a fraud?"

Consider what it will cost you.

How beneficial is that thought? Does it serve your values? Or does it cost more than it is worth?

Is this a good investment? Or is it merely just a fleeting thought dressed-up as a useful truth?

I am not suggesting that you undertake this internal enquiry with ever single thought that passes through your head. That is not going to leave you much time to get on with living the life you love! However, you can use this exercise every now and again, particularly with thoughts that make a regular appearance, or that seem to hang around for too long.

The more you use this exercise, along with the others in this chapter, the more you will naturally and effortlessly take an observer's perspective on your thoughts and be less likely to get tangled up in them.

CHAPTER NINE

Flip Those Feelings

'You hurt where you care, and you care where you hurt.'[16]

Steven C. Hayes made an invaluable observation when he wrote that pain and purpose are two sides of the same thing.[17] He notes that we would be unlikely to hurt over something we did not care about.

In a quest to help clients see how their pain relates to their values, Hayes states:

---

16 Steve Hayes, *A Liberated Mind*, p. 22.

17 Ibid.

> 'I tell them that as they open up to pain they should flip it over and ask, "What would I have to not care about for this not to hurt?" I've never met a person with social phobia who did not deeply desire to be with people in an open way. I've personally never met a person with depression who did not deeply desire to be vigorously engaged in life again. In your pain you find your values.'

That question - *What would I have to not care about for this not to hurt?* - is highly significant. Not only does it serve Hayes' goal of clarifying values, it also gives us another perspective to see our emotional pain from. Pain, it turns out, can be useful.

I am not suggesting that we 'always look on the bright side of life,' or that we should enthusiastically embrace our unpleasant thoughts, feelings and experiences because they are actually good *incognito*. Not at all. Being diagnosed with stage 4 cancer, or losing a loved one in a car crash, having a miscarriage, or being violently assaulted are unlikely to ever feel as if they are actually good events in and of themselves. Even if it is true that every cloud has a silver lining, that does not mean that we can always see it, or have the current capacity to look for it.

Recognising that our unpleasant thoughts, feelings and emotions can be useful to us is not an act of approval. It is, however, a case of acknowledging the reality of our situation. To use a rather simple practical example, if you lead an active life the idea of breaking your leg and spending six weeks in a cast may seem completely unbearable. Yet, as you sit there in a cast, it does no one any benefit to ruminate over what you could have been doing instead, if you had not broken your leg.

The reality is, you *have* broken your leg. Now, what are you going to do?

You might realise that you now have some time to start working on that book you never seem to get round to. Or you might discover that more of your job than you imagined can be completed virtually.

Brian Ogawa makes a similar point when he is discussing the exam anxiety that some of his students might suffer:

> 'I tell students to *appreciate* anxiety because it is an ally of their goal to learn. They should exploit the anxiety to reinforce their focus on study... The indifferent students are stress-free because they do not invest in their performance on the exam... Anxiety serves as a "cue" for translating desire for healthy and constructive living into concrete behaviours.'[18]

18 Brian Ogawa, *Desire for Life*, p. 95.

If we suppress, deny or resist our unpleasant feelings, we thus lose the opportunity to 'exploit' them in service of a valued action.

What Can you Learn?

Acceptance can thus involve seeking to learn all you can from unwanted feelings or experiences. This is not meant to imply any kind of spiritual intention behind why you had the experience. We are in no place to make such universal declarations. It is simply a recognition that we can very often come to realisations and fresh perspectives via experiences we may not have chosen.

This does not mean that the gods, or the Universe, or whomever sent you this experience in order to learn a specific lesson. However, reflection on our unwanted experiences can frequently uncover unexpected lessons about ourselves, others and the world as we know it.

One of the most common lessons we might learn is expressed in the quote which opened this chapter. Pain can often be a vital signal to remind us to take a look at our values. It may be that we are living out-of-step with our values and the pain that we are feeling is because of an internal sense of disconnect with those things that we hold most dear.

Alternatively, the pain may serve to reassure us that we are living in-line with our values. For example, we could be nervous about asking someone for a date because we value treating people with respect, or because we are keen to have an intimate partner with whom we can rediscover a sense of fun. So, at times, our pain can be a confirmation that we are heading in the right direction. We only hurt because we care.

How Can you Grow?

Another question we might ask as we exploit our pain is, "how can I grow through this?" The Christian scholar and beloved author C.S. Lewis described pain as the tool that God uses to chip away at blocks of stone (humanity), to reveal a masterpiece.

We may not agree that there is an intelligent intentional design behind our pain, though some certainly seem to find that idea helpful. However, even if we doubt a divine purpose behind our unpleasant experiences, how we utilise them can make them meaningful.

It may be that the pain reveals some skills or resources we are lacking. If so, we can use that pain as a motivation to address the matter. For example, we may have a fear of snakes that shows us we do not know much about them, or how to tell dangerous ones from their rather harmless counterparts. The pain then motivates us to seek more education on the matter.

Alternatively, the pain itself could be a means of developing or uncovering a means of growth. Perhaps a period of grief enables us to learn to stop trying to smother our emotions. Or heartbreak over a failed relationship may help us with being more vulnerable.

This is Not an Excuse to Escape

There is something that we need to be aware of here. We might sometimes encounter the temptation to 'flip' our feelings as a means of avoiding them. Don't fall for it. It's a trap!

The only way for us to learn from our pain, or grow through it, is to experience it. We do not disregard the cloud to find the silver lining; we embrace the whole.

Some criticisms of approaches like Morita Therapy presume that it is dismissive of feelings. They consider Morita to be saying, "I don't care what you're feeling. That's irrelevant. Get on and do something!" In reality, nothing could be further from the truth.

Morita therapy teaches us not to fight our feelings, or attempt to control them. Instead, we coexist with them. We do not allow them to dictate what we do, or detract us from our valued direction in life. However, we do not deny them either. We accept our emotions and then get on with living life – and feelings are a natural part of that.

***

Maria was an elderly client of mine, living with chronic pain. She suffered from arthritis, sciatica and migraines. Maria had contacted me to see if hypnotherapy could help reduce her number of migraines.

When I met Maria, she was hunched over and almost audibly creaked as she walked. Intrigued, I asked her why she was only asking for support with her migraines and not general pain management for all of her "bodily woes," as she called them.

"Well, I just figured you've got to have some pain in your life," she said.

I smiled at her words and her outlook on life. I initially thought she was being overly stoic, but as I spent more time with her, I learned that Maria had a rather unique perspective on things.

Maria's late husband, Terry, had also suffered from arthritis. "He was much worse than me," Maria said, "and he got it fairly early on." She explained how Terry suffered from Alzheimer's in the last years of his life and how she was effectively his carer.

Maria said that after half a year of looking after Terry, she was physically and emotionally exhausted. She said that she longed to see Terry free from pain, partly for his own relief, but also so that she could get some rest. When he did finally pass away, Maria said that she felt guilty for ever looking forward to that day.

Then Maria looked me in the eyes and said it was only after Terry had passed that she realised how lucky she was. I asked what she meant and she said that she got to hold the man she loved close to her every single day. She got to meet his needs and hear all of his stories. She then explained that due to the Alzheimer's, she got to see a side of him that she would not otherwise have encountered.

"Sometimes, it was a bit like a time-machine. I got to meet him when he was younger. I got to see his soul laid bare. And I got to care for him on those days when it all became too much."

I worked with Maria on her migraines. She said that she didn't mind if I couldn't get rid of them completely; she just wanted to experience them less often. I smiled again at this remarkable woman and said, "I'll see what I can do."

A few weeks after her final session, Maria sent me a

letter. She said that she had not experienced a migraine yet and was delighted by this fact. Then she said she hoped I would be able to accept her gift, as an act of appreciation. I tipped the envelope and out fell a knitted bookmark (we had often talked of our mutual love of books).

Maria had sewed a sentence in the middle of the bookmark, that I had heard her say once before. It struck me as powerful the first time I heard it. Now, seeing it laid out before me, it seemed more profound than I had initially realised.

The words on the bookmark read: Don't Waste Your Sorrows.

***

Feelings are a natural part of life. Negative feelings are as natural as positive and should not be denied, ignored, or fought against.

Pain will come and pain will go. That much is inevitable. The question is, what are you going to do with yours?

Whatever you do, I would implore you – Don't waste your sorrows.

CHAPTER TEN

Summary So Far

We have spent our time looking at 4 schools of therapy: ACT, DBT, MBSR and Morita Therapy. In doing so, we have drawn out a number of ideas, principles and practices that form the basis of what I have come to call *Brief Acceptance*.

We will next turn to consider 4 self-help methods that have acceptance at their core. Before we do that, let's summarise what we have learned so far.

***

We saw, at the beginning of the book, that Brief

Acceptance can give us the option of accepting a situation, even if it is just temporary.

We learned that our struggles in life often involve us fighting against reality. That is a battle we are never going to win.

Feelings are like 'mental weather.' We are not responsible for them and we cannot directly control them. We can, however, learn to live with them.

Our attempts to avoid any and all unpleasant experiences almost guarantee that we would experience them, for longer and stronger.

Practically every effective therapeutic method you can find contains at least some element of acceptance.

Ogawa, a Morita therapist, told us that 'We must accept the absolutely unchangeable to change the absolutely unacceptable.'

Acceptance is not indifference and does not mean approval or resignation. In some ways, Acceptance is simply about starting where you are.

This present moment—and your past experience—cannot be any different than it is. Wishing it was otherwise is simply an act of denial.

It turns out that the effort we put into avoiding

suffering, pain, and the struggles of life is only the cause of more suffering and more pain and itself a struggle.

The ultimate goal of Brief Acceptance is not symptom removal, but empowering you to live the life you love.

From ACT, we learned how important it can be to live life in accordance with our values. We also saw that Morita and others might question if this needs to lead to goal-setting, or if it is not more about following your passion.

MBSR taught us a series of exercises to work through. We discovered that there is what we might call formal mindfulness (which looks more like meditation) and informal mindfulness (which involves everyday mindful practices, such as eating, drawing or walking).

From Morita therapy, we learned of the importance of where we place our attention. We saw that those things that we focus on have a tendency to increase in size and effect.

ACT taught us about the risks and ineffectiveness of experiential avoidance. We learned, thanks to the unwanted party guest, that standing guard to dictate which emotions can or cannot be let in simply means that we don't get to enjoy the party of life.

We saw that the opposite of experiential avoidance is to take a stance of openness and willingness to all of life, expanding the number and type of experiences that are acceptable to us.

DBT provided us with a series of *Distress Tolerance skills*. We learned that these might help internally toughen us up a little. That is not meant as a means of rejecting or fighting unwanted feelings. Instead, it strengthens us to live with feelings we might otherwise have avoided, or been knocked-off course by.

ACT taught us another valuable practice – creating some distance between your thoughts and how easily we get entangled up in them. Through various exercises, we can be trained to not automatically and unquestionably believe or obey the thoughts that pop into our heads.

Finally, from both Morita therapy and ACT, we discovered that our painful emotions are often the flip-side of values or purposes that are important to us. We can therefore 'exploit' our pain to learn or grow – and keep on moving in the direction we have chosen.

***

If you have read the book – and followed the exercises – up to this point, I hope you have found some of these ideas and techniques as exciting as I do. You might be seeing a light at the end of the tunnel and the beginning of hope. Or you may already have experienced some of the transformation that Brief Acceptance can bring to our lives.

My contact details are at the end of the book and I would invite any readers with stories to share to get in touch with me.

We are now going to turn our attention to three very well-known self-help methods. In my opinion, they all include acceptance as a core component. We will then look at the B.A.T. process, which is a method I have developed, built upon Brief Acceptance principles.

All 4 of these methods help to demonstrate how fighting against reality is often the real cause of our pain. As with the rest of the book, you are invited to engage with them practically.

So, if you are ready, strap yourself in. The second stage of our journey could get bumpy!

CHAPTER ELEVEN

Happiness is an Option

The Option Method

Some time prior to 1970, Bruce Di Marsico created the Option Method when he came to realise that people were unhappy because they believed they "should" be.

According to Di Marsico, the driving belief inherent in unhappiness works like this:

> "If I wasn't unhappy about this, it would mean that I wanted it to happen."

Or,

> "If I wasn't sad (or angry, etc.), it would mean I didn't care."

To demonstrate his finding that unhappiness operated in this manner, Di Marsico developed two simple questions:

> "If you believed that at this time tomorrow you were going to be unhappy, what would you feel now?"

And,

> "If you were to believe now that at this time tomorrow you were going to become very happy, what would you feel now?"

The second belief listed above - "If I wasn't sad, it would mean I didn't care" - fits neatly with our finding in *Flip Those Feelings*. We hurt where we care. The difference with the Option Method is that it teaches that we do not need to hurt as a result of caring.

This similarity and difference between the Option Method and other Brief Acceptance methods may require a small explanation before we proceed any further.

An Open Dialogue with the Option Method

I would invite the reader to think of this chapter as an open dialogue with the Option Method. I do not intend to recommend the Option Method as a perfect example of a Brief Acceptance approach. In fact, we will see that there are some places where the two take opposing views of a situation.

So, what I aim to do in this chapter is examine the Option Method in the light of what we have seen so far in this book. I am effectively holding it up to the light and asking how it compares. I would invite you to consider it carefully, alongside what you have already read.

Could the Option Method work as a Brief Acceptance tool? Does it truly have acceptance at its core? Can it be partly incorporated in Brief Acceptance without us having to agree with all of it?

On the whole, I am going to leave it up to you how you answer those questions. I may offer my opinions here and there, but it is down to you to decide for yourself if the Option Method deserves a place in your Brief Acceptance tool-kit.

The Myth of Unhappiness

One of the core beliefs of the Option Method is that

happiness is our natural state. Uniquely, it states that we do not need to spend so much time and energy trying to be happy. All we need to do is address the causes of our *un*happiness.

The cause of unhappiness, according to Di Marsico is a belief. Events do not cause our unhappiness. Instead, it is how we respond to those events – with the belief that we should not be happy about them – that is the only cause of unhappiness.

This understanding of unhappiness is elaborated upon in *The Myth of Unhappiness*:

> Let's say you have a situation of a young girl going off to college. She's out in front of her home with her mother, her father, her younger sister, and there's a stranger passing on the sidewalk. And she's saying goodbye to them and she's going to college. Her mother is very distraught and very unhappy; there are tears in her eyes; she's feeling very sad. She's going to miss her daughter. She believes that what's happening is really kind of bad; she can't understand why she has to go away to school – there's a perfectly good school in town. Why she has to leave her family, etc. And the mother sees the situation pretty much as something that's to be unhappy about. And so she feels unhappy about it.

Her father on the other hand is kind of mixed. He feels that he's going to miss his little girl a little bit and he kinda wishes she was staying home; he was just getting to know her and they were just becoming friends. But he also sees that she's going to be off with her friends at a school that she's very much looking forward to being at, and how it's going to be really helpful to her for her maturity and her intellectual growth. And so in a way he's kind of glad too; he's a little sad and he's a little glad that she's going away. And of course the younger sister is overjoyed! She's just imagining having the room all to herself now, and the telephone all to herself, and nothing could be better than her big sister going off to College. And the stranger feels nothing and just walks by.

Now I use that to show you that there's one event taking place: A young woman going off to college is the event. And yet there are four different emotional reactions to that... How do we explain that?

We explain it by saying that the event in itself was just an event. The feelings about the event are based on the judgements about the event... So that if we believe a thing to be good, we feel good; if we believe it to be bad, we feel bad.[19]

19 Bruce Di Marsico, *The Myth of Unhappiness*, Vol. 1, pp. 7-8.

There are many schools of thought that would echo similar sentiments. For example, in the first century CE, Epictetus made a number of statements which serve as precursors of Di Marsico's thought:

> It's not what happens to you, but how you react to it that matters.
>
> Men are disturbed not by things, but by the view which they take of them.
>
> What really frightens and dismays us is not external events themselves, but the way in which we think about them. It is not things that disturb us, but our interpretation of their significance.

Similarly, Albert Ellis, the developer of *Rational Emotive Behaviour Therapy*, wrote:

> Too many people are unaware that it is not outer events or circumstances that will create happiness; rather, it is our perception of events and of ourselves that will create, or uncreate, positive emotions.[20]

However, the thinking or belief that the Option Method is most interested in is a specific one. It is the

---

20 Ellis, A., & Ellis, D. (2019). Introduction. In *Rational Emotive Behavior Therapy* (pp. 3-8). Washington, DC: American Psychological Association.

belief that you *should* be unhappy about this situation because it should not be happening. In other words, this is a bad situation and therefore you should feel bad about it.

Unhappiness, therefore, is nothing other than the belief that you should not be happy. As Di Marsico states, if a person did not believe he or she had to be unhappy, they would not and could not be.[21]

The Option Method Questions

The questions used in the Option Method are a means of identifying and clarifying our beliefs. Specifically, they are aimed at examining our 'hidden' beliefs about the fact that we *should* be unhappy.

The questions are:

1) What are you unhappy about?

2) What is it about that, that makes you unhappy?

3) Why are you unhappy about that?

4) What are you afraid it would mean if you were not unhappy about that?

5) Why do you believe it would mean that?

21 Bruce Di Marsico, *The Myth of Unhappiness*, p. 81.

Why not try this out for yourself right now? To begin, start with where you are, not where you want to get to, or think that you should be. Sit openly and willingly with your feelings and proceed as follows.

1) "What am I unhappy about?"

The word 'unhappy' can be replaced with any negative emotion you're feeling, as it is used to reference any unpleasant or unwanted feelings.

Then clarify your answer. Get as concrete and specific as you can. If your initial answer is something like, "I'm worried about my health," that is likely to be too broad an answer to be helpful. You need to narrow it down and be as specific as possible. The second question helps you to do that.

2) "What is it about that, that makes me unhappy?"

Using the example of "worrying about my health," you would now ask yourself, "What is it about my health that I am worried about?" You are aiming to be as specific as possible here. Another way of asking this question is, "What about my health worries me the most?" Your answer might be something like, "I'm going to become sick if I don't change how I'm living."

3) "Why am I unhappy about that?"

This question prompts us to recognize that we have

our own personal reasons for feeling the way we do. (In this context, "Why" means "for what reason.") Option Method aficionados would suggest that this question is a good way of reminding ourselves that we are not feeling the way we do against our will.

To apply this question to our example you would ask, "Why am I worried about getting sick?" At some point, you will probably find yourself feeling as if you don't know why. Perhaps you have just always been unhappy about it. Or, maybe it would seem unnatural to be happy in such circumstances.

4) "What am I afraid it would mean if I were *not* unhappy about that?"

Another way of asking this question is, "What am I afraid would happen if I were not unhappy about that?" This can be a powerful question. Take your time.

You may answer this question with something like, "It would mean I didn't care," or "It would mean I was crazy." Or to use our example, you may answer, "If I wasn't worried about being sick I'm afraid that I wouldn't do anything to improve my lifestyle and health."

Now is the time for the final question:

5) "Why do you believe it would mean that?"

In other words,

"Why do I believe that being happy would be bad for me right now?"

When it comes to our bad or undesirable feelings, the operating principles are fundamentally the same. If you believe something is bad, you feel bad about it. If you believe something is good, you feel good about it. If you believe that something is neither good nor bad, you don't have any feelings one way or the other. Most importantly, if you believe that if you were to feel happy in any given situation that it would be bad for you somehow, then naturally, you won't feel good.

Working through the questions in this way can bring to light the beliefs behind our unpleasant feelings and unhappiness. It is thought that we each have our own, individual, specific, reasons for getting unhappy when we do. The Option Method Questions are designed to help identify those reasons.

Do We Choose To Be Unhappy?

One of the more startling statements that you might hear from practitioners of The Option Method is that we can choose to be happy, just as we choose to be unhappy. However, is that a reliable description of what is taking place, even if we accept the Option model of happiness and unhappiness?

My suspicion is that this sort of terminology is used because it grabs the reader's attention. At the very least, we have to concede that the choosing that is being spoken of here is not a typical use of the word.

If my hand accidentally touches a hot stove, I will almost certainly remove it immediately. No one else does it for me. I remove my hand. Yet, I don't think anyone would say that I *chose* to move my hand. I doubt many people would even say that I was responsible for my hand being taken off of the stove. Nevertheless, I moved it.

Whilst working through the Option Method questions can elicit moments of genuine revelation – about our beliefs, fears, values and more – they also demonstrate that we often make 'decisions' about how we are going to feel regarding an event at a level far below our conscious awareness. I have to say, it feels like a stretch to call that a choice.

On the other hand, if we go through the Option Method questions and discover that there is a specific faulty belief underlying some of our anxiety, we could be expected to address that belief and resolve the anxiety. If we decline to do that, might we be said to be choosing to remain anxious?

One reason why Option may phrase things as it does

(aside from grabbing our attention) could be found in its intention to hand responsibility back to us. Option teachers are keen to remind us that we are not victims of our emotions. In fact, in their view, we play a vital part in creating our feelings.

Whilst we certainly can play a role in developing some unwanted emotions – for example, if we spend all day ruminating on a past mistake, we are unlikely to feel good in the evening – this does not mean we are responsible for all of our feelings. Option teachers do not like that assertion as it would seem to make us helpless victims.

I would respond by stating that I have never heard any practitioners of Morita therapy (or other acceptance-based methods) suggest that we are victims of our emotions. Our emotions and feelings just are. Option says our feelings do not happen to us, as if we are passive cogs in the system. Instead, we select those feelings through how we believe we should feel in a situation.

Morita therapy does not teach that our feelings happen to us either. It teaches that they happen. It then asks the vital question – *What are you going to do now?*

What Do You Think of The Option Method?

So, what's the verdict? Do you think that the Option Method is compatible with Brief Acceptance? Does it contradict or oppose any of the core components of the Brief Acceptance methods we have looked at so far?

Some of the areas where the two approaches might clash are the underlying philosophies. As just one example, the Option Method states that happiness is our natural state. Morita therapy, for example, would state that the natural state is one in which all manner of feelings come and go like the weather.

One of the areas where there may be significant similarities is the idea that there may be a reason or purpose to our feelings. Option might help us see where a feeling serves us well, or where it is creating a blockage of some kind, preventing the natural ebb and flow.

A somewhat surprising omission from the Option Method is any discussion of the potential desirability of emotional pain. If we can compare physical pain with emotional pain, when a woman is giving birth to a child, is that pain wrong? Can that pain be welcomed at all? Would all women describe giving birth as a bad experience, due to the pain involved?

Is all emotional pain to be avoided, or conquered in some way? If we were told in advance that a new life was on the way, would some emotional pain be considered acceptable?

I have suggested that it is in the underlying philosophy – for example, the belief that we are responsible for our feelings – that the Option Method might not fit well with other Brief Acceptance models. However, if we look even deeper than that, as what might be considered its core assumption, we might find that acceptance is behind it all:

The Option Method states, fundamentally, that it is the belief that you *should* be unhappy about a situation – because it should not be happening – that is the cause of your unhappiness.

Does this not mean that the real issue with unhappiness, according to this model, is a failure to accept reality as it is?

We 1) feel that a situation should not be happening and 2) we believe that we should not be happy about that, 3) so we are unhappy.

The Option Method would address this unhappy loop at number 2. That is, *our beliefs about how we should feel.* Yet, can we not go deeper and challenge the belief found in the first point, that *a situation should not be happening*?

Unhappiness would appear to exist because we cannot accept both a situation and our feelings about that situation. In that sense, could acceptance be the most useful option of all?

Using the Option Method

One of the refreshing things about Brief Acceptance is that it does not exist simply to make us feel better. It is instead focused on liberating us to live a valued life. Many self-help tools imply that once we have removed a particular problem, or can feel a certain way, then we can get on with living. Brief Acceptance suggests that it is actually the other way round.

You do not need to remove all unpleasant feelings or emotional pain to live the life you love. In fact, getting on and living that life may be one of the most effective things you can do to address the pain.

However, we are not stoic for the sake of it. It is simply a question of focus and what we pay attention to. Yet, as Shoma Morita said, if it is raining and you have an umbrella, use it.

The Option Method – along with the other self-help tools we will turn to shortly – can be thought of as one of your umbrellas.

If a particular emotional experience is unacceptable to you, then – if you are able to – change it.

Or, if a specific emotion keeps on cropping-up and it diverts you from your chosen direction, then - where possible – change it.

With the Option Method, you now have a powerful tool for change, albeit one with acceptance at its core!

CHAPTER TWELVE

Working with What is

"I discovered that when I believed my thoughts, I suffered, but when I didn't believe them, I didn't suffer, and that this is true for every human being."[22]

The Work, developed by Byron Katie, is often described as "Four Questions and a Turnaround." However, I prefer the description that one of my clients gave it – CBT on steroids! Even so, I am beginning this chapter with a word of warning.

---

22 Byron Katie.

Proceed With Caution

We will be looking at The Work as an acceptance-based self-help tool. Many people have found it to be a powerful and beneficial method. Yet, our discussion of The Work is not meant to be an endorsement of Byron Katie, or a promotion of her books, speaking events or general views *in any way whatsoever.*

Katie claims that The Work came to her in a split-second of revelation when she was at rock bottom, in a halfway house for women. However, other sources have questioned this and even stated that some of the books she read there contained ideas identical to The Work. One author that Katie apparently read even called his method The Inner Work!

More troubling than Katie apparently passing off someone else's work as her own are stories of some of her behaviour at her events. Some attendees speak of an almost cult-like atmosphere, with Katie lauded as an unquestionable and infallible guru. Unfortunately, this means that some of her actions and statements go unchallenged.

This is not the place for me to write a thorough critique or analysis of Byron Katie. However, I felt it was necessary for me to make a distinction between The Work and the person behind it. I am only discussing the former in this chapter.

What is The Work?

The Work is a method of self-inquiry. It is a simple, yet powerful, set of questions that we can ask ourselves regarding any specific belief or thought that is causing us pain.

You write down the thought or belief that you want to work on and then ask yourself the following questions:

1. Is it true?
2. Can you absolutely know that it's true?
3. How do you react when you believe that thought?
4. Who would you be without the thought?

The questions are then followed by a 'turnaround,' a way to consider alternative perspectives and reflect on them.

Let's unpack this a little, before you try it out for yourself.

Question 1: Is it true?

Be still and ask yourself if the thought you wrote down is true. There is no correct answer. If you say "no" in response to this question, jump to question 3.

Question 2: Can you absolutely know it's true?

Ultimately, can you really know with 100% certainty that your thought is true?

Question 3: How do you react—what happens—when you believe that thought?

With this question, you begin to notice that when you believe the thought it is unpleasant for you. How do you feel? Do you experience anger, stress, or frustration? How do you respond? How do you treat other people or yourself when you believe that thought? Be specific.

Question 4: Who would you be without the thought?

Imagine how your life would be different if you didn't have the ability to even think that thought? How would you feel? Which do you prefer – life with or without the thought?

The Turnaround

The turnaround provides you with an an opportunity to experience the opposite of what you believe. So, for example, "Annie is so impatient," could become, "*I* am so impatient," or, "Annie is so *patient*."

Once you have found one or more turnarounds, it is a good idea to come up with at least three specific, genuine examples of how each turnaround is true in your life.

This is not about blaming yourself or feeling guilty. It's about discovering alternatives that can bring you peace. If the turnaround does not seem to be true, or does not bring you any more peace than your initial thought, then pick another one.

To clarify things further, I will provide an example of when I used The Work on some feelings of resentment. After that, I will invite you to road-test it for yourself.

***

I once shared office space with another therapist who had the gift of the gab and some dubious qualifications along with it. When the local newspaper or radio station were looking for a comment from a Well-being expert, they would often seek him out.

I could live with that, because he did talk a good game. However, I really struggled to accept things when I learned that the Newspaper wanted to write a piece about him and his methods. I just could not seem to get past the idea that it should have been me they wanted to write about.

So, I used The Work on the statement, "It should be me getting the attention."

1. Is that true?

Yes. It seems obvious to me that I am more deserving of media attention than him.

2. Can you absolutely know that it's true?

Well, no, I can't know for certain. It definitely feels *true though.*

3. How Do You React, What Happens, When You Believe That Thought?

I can become quite obsessive with thinking negative thoughts about him. I pick up on the tiniest things he does and add them to my mental list of all the things he does wrong. I become judgemental and that often develops into a grumpy cynicism about anything and everything.

4. Who Would You Be Without That Thought?

I would be more positive, more focused on the good in people and rediscover that light joyful side of me that I haven't seen in a while.

The Turnaround:

It should be him *getting the attention.*

It could *be me getting the attention*

It should not *be me getting the attention.*

As I reflected upon it, the third statement – It should not be me getting the attention – *actually felt surprisingly good. I had no desire to be a celebrity therapist and I would prefer to be able to go shopping without people pointing and saying, "He's that quack from the paper." I valued being left alone to do my job and would not want anything jeopardising that, or eating into my family time.*

One of the outcomes of my self-inquiry on this issue was that I rediscovered an element of passion for the work that I did. I found myself re-focusing on my client's and their needs and goals. The lack of an ambition to make a name for myself was incredibly liberating.

***

Now it's your turn!

Write down a statement, thought or belief that has been causing you some distress. Then ask yourself the four questions. Be honest, be specific and take your time.

When it comes to the turnaround, the idea is to see how it feels to hold an opposite thought to the one that is painful for you. However, where this is not possible, I recommend playing around with different perspectives, as if you are holding it up to the light and inspecting it from all sides. You might not find an opposite statement that works for you, but there may be some others that you discover along the way.

So, here goes:

1. Is it true?
2. Can you absolutely know that it's true?
3. How do you react when you believe that thought?
4. Who would you be without the thought?

   The Turnaround.

The Mechanism behind The Work

How did you find that? Were you able to come up with alternative beliefs that felt easier to keep hold of? Or did you find yourself less tied to the original thought as you worked through the questions? Perhaps you simply found that your initial statement is no longer as troubling as it once was.

It would be interesting at this point to consider how The Work functions. And I'm guessing you wouldn't be surprised to hear me say that I believe The Work relies upon acceptance!

In some ways, The Work functions along the same lines as some of the defusion exercises we looked at earlier. It allows you to question whether the thoughts you've been holding are a true reflection of reality. In the same way, it prompts you to step back and consider whether any of your thoughts are 100% accurate. That is, it teaches us not to believe everything we think.

The Work is a way to identify and question the thoughts that cause you pain. These thoughts are always expressions of your desire for reality to be different than it is. They are a reflection of your dissatisfaction with reality.

As we work through the questions and experiment with a number of turnarounds, we can find an unexpected clarity and peace within us. When we find peace with ourselves and our (inner and outer) world, we find the freedom to fully embrace reality.

CHAPTER THIRTEEN

Emotional Freedom

For a good number of years, colleagues of mine would praise the effectiveness of the Emotional Freedom Technique (EFT) and I would half-jokingly roll my eyes at them. I just could not bring myself to take EFT seriously, as I was not able to get passed the alleged "science" behind it.

Yet, there was no denying that the anecdotal evidence for the effectiveness of this technique is through the roof. As I began to listen more closely to the first-hand accounts of success with EFT, I also discovered that there was actually significant academic support for the effectiveness of the technique.[23]

So, I am now at a point where I incorporate EFT into my clinical work, whilst still being something of a sceptic! As well as using EFT in my sessions, I also teach it to some clients as "home-work" for them to do between sessions.

The Emotional Freedom Technique

The Emotional Freedom Technique, or "Tapping," was developed by Gary Craig as an off-shoot of Roger Callaghan's original 'Thought-field Therapy.' Both of the techniques share a belief that physical pain and emotional distress are experienced due to blockages in the body's meridian channels.

According to Craig, EFT works by tapping on certain pre-defined areas of the body – considered to be points along the meridian pathway – whilst repeating a statement. These points generally correspond to those used in traditional acupuncture and acupressure.

Let me be clear about this: I believe that EFT works. I believe that it it can be incredibly effective. Yet, I believe that is more down to the statements used than any other reasons espoused by its practitioners.

---

23 See, for example. *The Science Behind Tapping* by Peta Stapleton.

As you will see, EFT incorporates elements of a) exposure therapy, b) acceptance of your experience and feelings and c) acceptance of yourself.

The Tapping Points

Below, we will illustrate the 9 tapping points used in basic EFT.

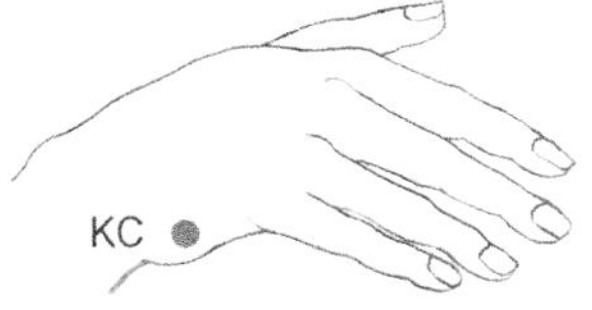

The Karate-Chop (or KC) point is the one you will begin with, where you will tap out your phrase (seen below) in its fullest.

The following 8 points – for which you will only be using a reminder phrase – are shown in the diagram below.

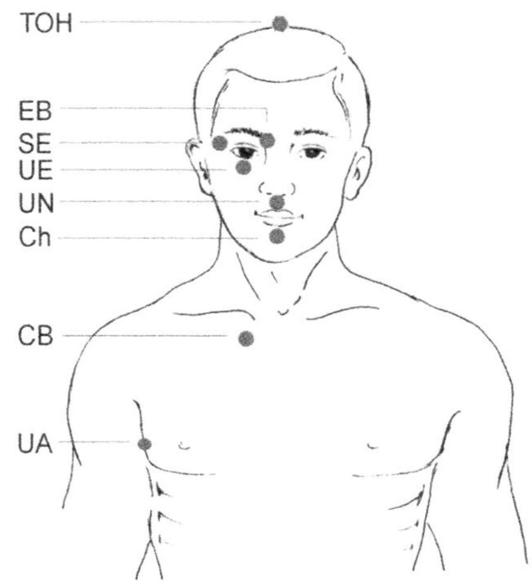

The 5 Steps of The EFT Tapping Basic Recipe

1. Identify the Issue

This may be anxiety you are currently feeling or, for example, a past event that you cannot stop ruminating over. This becomes the target at which you "aim" the tapping. Be sure you are only targeting one issue at a time.

2. Test the Initial Intensity

Here you measure the issue's starting intensity by assigning a number to it on a 0-10 scale, where 10 is the worst the issue has ever been and 0 is no problem whatsoever. This serves as a benchmark so you can compare your progress after each round of EFT.

For past events, you can recreate the memory in your mind and assess the level of discomfort. For anxiety or phobias, you could scale any anxiety you currently feel, or think of the specific thought that arouses your anxiety and then measure the intensity.

3. The Set-up

The Set-up is a process used to start each round of Tapping. By designing a simple phrase and saying it whilst continuously tapping the KC point (see above), you effectively let your body and mind know what you are intending to focus upon and address.

When designing this phrase there are two goals to achieve:

- Acknowledge the problem
- Accept yourself in spite of it

You do this by saying:

"Even though I have this ________, I deeply and completely accept myself."

The blank line represents the problem you want to

address, so you can just insert things like:

> *This fear of spiders:*
>
> "Even though I have this fear of spiders, I deeply and completely accept myself."
>
> *The humiliation at last year's Xmas party:*
>
> "Even though I have this humiliation from last year's Christmas party, I deeply and completely accept myself."
>
> *This current anxiety:*
>
> "Even though I have this current anxiety, I deeply and completely accept myself."

Not all of the issues will fit neatly into "Even though I have this ____," so you can use some flexibility when designing your phrase. However, by using "Even though I have this ____," you will naturally choose something that represents your experience, your reaction, or a problem that you recognize as something that belongs to you, and that is a significant live issue for you.

4. The Sequence

This is the gist of The EFT process, which hard-core enthusiasts feel stimulates, unclogs or balances the body's energy pathways. To perform it, you tap each of the points shown in the Points diagram above whilst saying a Reminder Phrase that keeps you tuned-in to the issue. The points are repeated below, followed by a description of the Reminder Phrase:

- Top of the Head (TOH)
- Beginning of the Eyebrow (EB)
- Side of the Eye (SE)
- Under the Eye (UE)
- Under the Nose (UN)
- Chin Point (CH)
- Beginning of the Collarbone (CB)
- Under the Arm (UA)

The Reminder Phrase is quite simple as you need only identify the issue with some brief wording. Depending on your issue, you might say the following at each tapping point:

"This fear of spiders,"

"Current anxiety,"

"Humiliation at last year's Christmas party."

5. Test the Intensity Again

Finally, after having gone through all of the points, you scale once again, from 0-10. You compare this with the initial scale to see how much progress you have made.

If you are not down to zero, then repeat the process until you either achieve zero or plateau at some level. Some people choose to switch to the EFT Intentions method (described later in this chapter) after two or three sequences.

Tapping Tips

Some of the Tapping points have twin points on each side of the body. For example, the "eyebrow" point on the right side of the body has a twin point on the left side of the body. Most practitioners agree that you only need to tap one of these twin points.

You can also switch sides when you tap these points. For example, during the same round of The EFT Tapping Basic Recipe, you can tap the "karate chop" point on your *left* hand and the eyebrow point on the *right* side of your body. Most people find that this makes the Tapping process more convenient to perform.

The Tapping is done with two or more fingertips. This is so you can cover a larger area and thereby ensure that your Tapping covers the correct point.

While you can tap with the fingertips of either hand, most people use their dominant hand. For example, right-handed people tap with the fingertips of their right hand, while left-handed people tap with the fingertips of their left hand.

You tap approximately 5 times on each point. There is no need to count the taps because anywhere between 3 and 7 taps on each point is fine. The only exception is during the Set-up step, where the Karate Chop Point is tapped *continuously* whilst you repeat the Set-up phrase.

The process is easily memorized. After you have tapped the Karate Chop Point, the rest of the points simply go down the body. The Eyebrow point, for example, is below the Top of the Head point. The Side of the Eye point is below the Eyebrow point. And so on, down the body.

The EFT Intentions Method

Some people find that they respond more effectively to the *EFT Intentions Method* than standard EFT.[24] This is especially true if they are dealing with issues of low self-esteem and/or self-acceptance. The words, "I deeply and completely accept myself" can be a barrier for such people, making the entire process feel like a pretence.

The usual advice is to still use the words if at all possible. The theory seems to be that by employing them as a positive affirmation, you will be training yourself and readjusting your balance in the process. However, this may not work so well for those people for whom such language feels a little forced or unnatural. So, for some people with genuine issues around self-acceptance, the EFT process could become a reinforcement of feelings of failure and generate negative rather than positive energy.

---

24 The EFT Intentions Method is my variation on the EFT Choices method. In the latter, the choice would tend to be an affirmation of some kind. E.g. "Even though I have this fear, I choose to feel calm and confident." However, I prefer to make the choice a statement of intent – an action to be carried out. This approach fits nicely with Brief Acceptance.

My first suggestion would be to soften the acceptance part of the phrase. Instead, you might say something like, "Even though I'm anxious about my interview, I accept myself and how I feel."

Having said that, you may encounter some issues, where the language of "I deeply and completely accept myself" might just seem irrelevant. In such situations, the EFT Intentions method may be the preferred option.

The Set-up Phrase

The only difference between basic EFT and the EFT Intentions method is the wording used. The process of tapping remains the same.

In this case, instead of saying:

> "Even though I have this current anxiety, I deeply and completely accept myself..."

You might say something more like:

> "Even though I have this current anxiety, I choose to hold my head high and enjoy socialising tonight."

It is important that the choice is not simply a contradiction of the problem. So, you would not say anything like, "Even though I have this current anxiety, I choose to not be anxious." Instead, you make a statement of intent. You accept the existence of the problem, but declare that it will not effect the choices or behaviours you carry out.

Your reminder phrase may still be "this current anxiety," for the first round of tapping. However, if the anxiety remains to some degree after re-scaling, I would suggest using your intention as the reminder phrase for the second round. Yet, bear in mind that unlike basic EFT, you are not focused on *completely* removing your anxiety, as that becomes unnecessary. You have announced your intention and will act on it regardless of any anxiety you do or do not feel.

Put it To The Test

Time to road-test this for yourself!

1. Identify your issue

When you are ready, begin by identifying an issue you want to address. This is what you will focus on during the tapping sequence.

2. Test the initial intensity

After you identify the issue or problem you want to work on, you need to measure your starting level of intensity. On a scale of 0 to 10, assesses the emotional or physical pain and discomfort you feel from the issue you are focusing on.

3. The setup

Establish a phrase that explains what you will be working on. It needs to have two main goals:

- acknowledging the issue(s)
- accepting yourself despite the issue

The common setup phrase is: "Even though I have this [issue or problem], I deeply and completely accept myself."

4. The tapping sequence

Begin by tapping the karate chop point while simultaneously reciting your setup phrase three times. Then, tap each of the following points three to seven times, moving down the body in this order:

- Top of the Head
- Beginning of the Eyebrow
- Side of the Eye
- Under the Eye
- Under the Nose

- Chin Point
- Beginning of the Collarbone
- Under the Arm

While tapping the ascending points, recite a reminder phrase (e.g. "this fear of flying") to maintain focus on your issue. Recite this phrase at each tapping point.

5. Scale the final intensity

At the end of your sequence, rate your intensity level on a scale from 0 to 10. Compare your results with your initial intensity level. If you have not reached zero, repeat the process until you do. Alternatively, after two or three sequences, you might choose to finish off with the EFT Intentions method.

Accepting Emotional Freedom

There are numerous theories regarding how and why EFT works. We have already seen the theories of Gary Craig and Roger Callahan before him. The idea that our meridian pathways can be blocked, causing negative emotions – which EFT helps to dislodge – is one that is also shared by many practitioners of EFT. However, it is not a necessary belief to hold in order to achieve successful outcomes with the technique.

For what it's worth, I will share my basic understanding of how EFT works, placing it firmly in the Brief Acceptance camp.[25]

When we begin with the initial scaling, it allows a brief moment of exposure to the troubling issue to be addressed. We only sample the source of our distress long enough to measure it.

Then, as we repeat our set-up phrase, we match together the feeling that our issue evokes in us along with a statement of acceptance of ourselves. However, you may have already noticed that by scaling our issue and then recalling it each time we make a statement of self-acceptance we are at least temporarily also accepting the issue or the feelings that it brings up.

As we repeat the reminder phrase with each act of tapping, we are effectively saying, "I accept myself whilst I feel this way." In doing so, we are effectively accepting the way that we feel and asserting that it does not change how we feel about ourselves. We accept ourselves as we currently are (meaning whilst we are experiencing negative feelings). We accept the version of ourselves that has the feelings it has.

---

25 Please note that this is a description of what is experienced by the client. For a more thorough scientific explanation of what is taking place 'under the surface' you might want to consult Peta Stapleton's *The Science Behind Tapping*.

Finally, the act of tapping creates a physical distraction that can function as a pattern-interrupt. We are used to i) thinking about our issue and ii) almost automatically feeling a particular way. Tapping loosens the link between the two by adding an additional sensation for your brain to focus on and process.

So, whilst tapping and trying to focus on your issue and the reminder phrase, you are actually doing a number of things simultaneously:

1. You are focusing on your issue
2. You are feeling the feelings that come up
3. You are accepting yourself even whilst feeling those feelings
4. You are focused on the physical sensation of tapping

In effect, you are re-training how your brain reacts to a specific stimuli. You condition yourself to doing something other than feeling bad when you recall a particular event. You learn that it is possible – and safe – to accept yourself, whilst still feeling the way you do. This makes the feeling less threatening and in turn reduces its negative impact.

There is more than this taking place during tapping

(including effects on our nervous system and the production of stress hormones), but I believe that labelling EFT as an example of Brief Acceptance is demonstrably valid and illuminating.

CHAPTER FOURTEEN

The BAT Process

We come now to the final self-help tool that we will be considering for our toolbox. I call this the Brief Acceptance and Transformation Process. Or, simply, the BAT.

My recommendation would be for you to read through this chapter first. Familiarise yourself with the process. Then work through an issue using the BAT.

In its most basic form, the BAT consists of the following 5 stages. (You'll notice that for ease of recall, the stages follow the order of vowels, AEIOU.)

1. Access
2. Externalise
3. Investigate
4. Overhaul
5. Utilise

What are we going to do?

This simple process that we are going to go through is something that I describe as being "verbal voodoo." Not that it actually has anything to do with genuine voodoo as a religion. I'm talking more of the stereotype of a voodoo doll that we might see in movies.

So you have these dolls that represent a person and you stick a pin in the doll and apparently the real person will feel it. In a similar way, we are going to come up with symbols or images or avatars or dolls to represent your thoughts and feelings. We are then going to play around with the symbol and just see what difference that makes to the feeling.

Think of it as an experiment. Let's see what happens.

Access

To start, you are going to access your feelings.

Now, I want you to know that you are perfectly safe. And this is a temporary step on the road to transformation.

So, I would invite you to think about the issue that is causing you difficulty. And as soon as you access the troublesome feelings, you can stop thinking about it, but keep hold of those feelings for a little bit longer.

As the thought fades away, you are left with just a physical feeling. It's only a feeling – nothing to fear.

I'm sure it's a feeling you are thoroughly familiar with. If not, take some time to get to know it. For the purposes of transformation, you might even think of yourself as welcoming the feeling. Get a handle on it, so you know what you will be working on.

And I can't help but wonder, "What would it mean if you did not have that feeling when you think about that? What would that mean to you?"

As you sit with those feelings, without judging them or avoiding them, I wonder if you can notice *where* in your body you can feel it.

And maybe you want to ask yourself if you are sure

that you want that feeling to change. And are you ready for that to happen now?

Externalise

We are now going to take that feeling and externalise it, outside of your body. The first step in doing that is to symbolise the feeling.

You might have already done this without realising, as you spent time noticing and locating the feeling. It might have seemed to have a certain shape, or to be a particular colour.

So, just clear your mind and ask your subconscious mind for a symbol that represents that old feeling you are working on. A symbol can be anything. It could be a beach ball, a coat hanger, or a kitten. It might be a pulsating blob of colour. It might even just be a sound, a smell, or a shape. Let your mind come up with whatever symbolises that feeling. The first thing that comes up – no matter how strange it might seem to your conscious mind – is usually the right one.

Now, just take a moment to familiarise yourself with that symbol. Really get to know it. Some things you might want to consider (though they might not all be relevant) are: Is it big or small? Is it solid or translucent? What colour is it? Is it still or moving? Light or heavy? Hard or soft? Cold, warm, or hot?

And when you have a symbol that represents how that issue made you feel, it is time to externalise it.

We are going to move your symbol outside of your body. You might imagine yourself taking hold of it and bringing it out of you. Or you may simply allow it to float out of your body, until it is about two feet in front of you.

When it is there, notice if externalising it has changed anything about it, e.g. it's size or shape. Now we are ready to move onto the next stage.

Investigate

With the symbol out in front of you, you can begin to inspect it more closely.

Turn the image around and upside down, so that you can observe it all. Bring it closer to you, or further away, if you want to get a better view of it.

Look at your symbol with compassion. This is, after all, an aspect of you.

The act of acknowledging all parts of you and your experience, may well enable you to become more whole. We can learn how sometimes the most despised, hidden or dismissed places within us contain our greatest treasures.

You could even ask questions that might seem

nonsensical, but that could serve you well. You may want to ask what the symbol needs. Is it lacking in some way, missing something important?

Does that symbol have anything to teach you? You may not consciously be aware of an answer – though you could be – but as your subconscious mind generated the symbol, you can trust your subconscious to pick up on any lessons that the symbol contains for you.

If you have an inkling of an answer to these questions, notice if that changes the feelings associated with your symbol.

Overhaul

Begin to play around with some of the symbol's features. (Some people find it helpful to imagine taking the symbol in their hands and adjusting it like a lump of clay.)

If it is cold, make it warm. If it is heavy, make it light. Change the colour, the shape, the texture. Make it bigger or smaller.

As you do this, notice any changes in the feeling the symbol contains. Do you prefer the new feelings, brought about by modifying the symbol, or would you rather keep the original feeling?

Continue to make changes to the shape, noticing the effect it has on your feelings. What happens if you send the symbol out into the distance? Or, how does it feel when you bring it closer?

When you've played around enough and discovered some beneficial changes you could make, it is now time to pass the steering wheel back to your subconscious mind. If you no longer want to feel the way that your original symbol represented, consider what you want to feel instead. For example, rather than saying, "I don't want to feel anxious," think about what you *do* want to feel. Calm? Confident? At peace?

Then invite your subconscious mind to continue to make any necessary changes to the symbol, until it captures what you want to feel instead of the old feeling. Your mind may do this instantly, or gradually. Keep allowing and noticing the changes until you find that your new shape represents your desired new feelings.

Utilise

Here is where we utilise any lessons learned, perspective gained, or changes made. You are going to take the symbol and put it back inside you, in its original place.

> **One word of advice**: if the symbol felt more pleasant when it was further away, see that as

> a trick of perception. Imagine getting hold of that distant symbol and as you bring it closer to you it retains the smaller shape it had when it was far away. It may even keep its blurred nature, or whatever else it took on when you moved it out.

Now simply place that symbol back inside and wiggle it around a bit until it is a nice secure fit. How does that more pleasant symbol feel inside you?

Take the new feelings that this symbol represents and feel them within you now. Then let that new feeling expand and spread across your body, throughout your entire being. Some people do this by imagining the shape expanding to fill them. Others imagine the shape glowing and spreading a bright light throughout their body. Simply go with whatever your subconscious mind comes up with and let those feelings spread.

What does it mean to you as you experience this now?

Check the Difference

For a moment, I want you to think of something completely different. It will seem like a strange request, but think of the colour of your front door, or imagine the smell of freshly baked pastries, sing a line or two from one of your favourite songs. You get the idea.

Once you have successfully changed your focus of attention, I am going to ask you to think again about the issue or incident that was troubling you. (Don't worry if the idea of doing that generates butterflies in your stomach at first. That is simply your mind getting excited at seeing the new response.)

Think about the issue that was causing you some difficulty. How do you feel now when you think about that? My hunch is that the feeling has changed, or you have somehow changed your relationship with the feeling and the issue behind it.

Now that you feel differently about the incident, can you tell me what you now *think* about it? What sort of new thoughts do you have that assist you to feel this way?

Is BAT a Tool for Change or Acceptance?

The question that sometimes crops up when someone first learns of the BAT process is: Is this a means of accepting something, or is it a tool for change? My experience of using BAT, both on myself and with clients, would suggest that it is both. At the very least, this is an exercise in *brief* acceptance. However, it also leads to change more often than not.

The nature of the transformation may not be a case of

symptom removal. However, feedback would suggest that you will almost certainly experience a change in your relationship to the issue and therefore the impact it has on you.

That might sound a little wishy-washy until you try it for yourself. Nevertheless, the simple act of acceptance is powerfully transformative. So, what better place to begin?

And that's your cue! You might want to read the chapter one more time, or get straight to it.

Here is a reminder of the stages:

1. **Access**
2. **Externalise**
3. **Investigate**
4. **Overhaul**
5. **Utilise**

I would love to hear how you get on with the BAT, so feel free to get in touch with any feedback after you have gone through the process.

CHAPTER FIFTEEN

But, but, but...

Doesn't acceptance lead to inaction?

If acceptance was simply a passive resignation, a case of rolling over in defeat and accepting whatever life throws at us, I could understand why people might view that as a cause of inaction. However, the truth is the exact opposite. The type of acceptance we are promoting in this book is fundamentally active and dynamic.

Acceptance is not about inaction or passivity. Rather, it is about acknowledging and recognising reality just as it is, in all its pain and glory. It is a state of fully embracing reality with clarity and non-judgemental attention. That is precisely the conditions from which effective action flows.

Ironically, it is non-acceptance that is passive. It teaches us that we are victims of our thoughts, feelings and circumstances. It leads us to believe that we can never move forward in life until the past is dealt with. Yet, that simply ensnares us in wrestling with reality. Our attention, focus and energy is then spent on avoiding unpleasant feelings, or grappling with the past.

Living the life you love becomes a secondary concern if non-acceptance is in the driving seat.

I just cannot accept it!

Brief Acceptance does not insist that you *must* accept every single thing that has happened to you. It simply gives you tools to discover that life generally is freer, more peaceful and more productive if you give up the struggle of fighting with reality.

There will be some situations where acceptance might not be beneficial. For example, the day after you have had a miscarriage, or the week after your spouse of 60 years has passed away. In such circumstances, it is natural to go through a grieving process, which positions acceptance at the very end.

If you are not in a situation like the above, or if you have been in that place for an extended length of time, you might want to reconsider the possibility and benefits of acceptance.

The bottom-line is, if you can continue living in an endless battle with reality, without it hampering your life, or dragging you down, then by all means do so. However, if you have a sense that you would be more able to lead the life you want to, if you were not stuck in a tug of war with events from the past, I would encourage you to begin working on your acceptance and distress tolerance skills.

If you desire to change the impact that the past is having on you, or break-free from events in the present, or simply clear the dust away so you can move forward into the future, then – by all means – change your situation if you are able to. However, even then, I would suggest that change starts with acknowledging where you are, along with the willingness to accepting your situation as it currently is. That way, you will be able to see your reality clearly, note what needs to be changed and begin to transform your life as you know it.

What about global injustice, or movements like Black Lives Matter?

We have already seen a quote from the Morita Therapist, Brian Ogawa. He succinctly wrote that 'We must accept the absolutely unchangeable to change the absolutely unacceptable.'[26]

The death of George Floyd was unchangeable after it happened. We can deny that painful truth and I'm sure many people would understand the motivation to do that. However, until we accept that George Floyd was brutally and unlawfully killed by Police officers, we will never be in a position to challenge and change the unacceptable.

Acceptance in a situation like this is not accepting that Police brutality towards people of colour happens and there is nothing we can do about it. That would be resignation. Neither would acceptance mean simply standing by and watching whilst Derek Chauvin kneeled on George Floyd's neck and ignored his pleas for help. That would be denial, not acceptance.

However, both to intervene whilst it is happening and to see clearly that there is ongoing systemic racism in many sectors of society requires firstly acknowledging the situation as it really is. It means accepting where

---

26 Ogawa, *A River to Live By*, p. 68.

we are in order to work to get us where we need to be.

As Carl Jung wrote, 'We cannot change anything until we accept it.'

Brief Acceptance is the perfect tool to enable you to accept things as they are, in order to change that which can – and therefore must – be changed.

You *can* change feelings directly!

One of the underlying assumptions of Morita Therapy is that we cannot change negative emotions through a direct act of the will. Given that we are talking about pragmatism, not absolute truth, we can perhaps soften the statement in Brief Acceptance and say something like, 'we cannot always change every negative emotion through a direct act of the will.'

Even then, I have been faced with objections, particularly from fellow therapists. One very confidently told me that he was sure he could change my mood from fed-up to happy in a split second. I pointed out that the question is not whether someone else can influence your mood, but if you can change it directly yourself by an act of the will. Nevertheless, I asked him to explain how he would change my mood and he said, "Easy. I'd show you a photo of a newborn baby smiling."

I conceded that such a photo would most likely change my mood. However, I went on to explain that such a change would not be guaranteed to work for all people at all times. Additionally, I said that it was not directly changing my mood through an act of will. There was an extra mediating step involved.

Finally, I informed my colleague that their example actually supported my claim, not theirs. I pointed out that if they showed me a photo of a smiling baby, I would likely not have control over my reaction. My mood would almost certainly improve, with no conscious intervention on my part. Therefore, it would serve to demonstrate that my thoughts and feelings are very often not something I can control or change at will.

This may be a good place to make an observation on this topic. Even if we were able to directly control our emotions through an act of the will, why would we want to? For starters, that would be exhausting! However, I also think we miss something if we make non-suffering a life goal. As implied in the chapter on flipping our feelings, negative emotions can often serve (or be made to serve) a positive purpose. I suspect that our lives would be dramatically less worthwhile if we removed all unpleasant feelings.

Do you really think I should just accept the dreadful thing that happened to me?

It should be remembered that acceptance is not the same thing as approval. It is simply acknowledging what has happened (or is happening) and making room for painful feelings and sensations.

The alternative is to carry on struggling with, or denying, the things you have been through. That does not make your life any easier, or help you move forward in life.

To continue to battle with the reality of what has happened only serves to increase and sustain the negative feelings it brings up for you. In effect, that means you keep the suffering you have experienced as a 'live issue' for you, causing you to suffer again and again and again.

No one is suggesting that you 'just' accept what has happened. Instead, you accept reality as a means of taking valued action. Acceptance means starting where you are, which is essential if you wish to address what has happened to you, by going to the Police, seeking counselling, or working towards change.

I don't like living without goals

Then don't! In our chapter on values, we provide a couple of ways to develop goals in line with your values. However, we also note that some people – particularly those holding a Moritist perspective – don't find goals to be as necessary or beneficial as countless Business and Life Coaching books would suggest.

If you are not one of those people and you feel that goals would work well for you, especially in living your valued life, then by all means set some goals. There is nothing about goal-setting that is necessarily against the spirit of Brief Acceptance.

What Is the Goal of Acceptance and Commitment Therapy?

The goal of ACT is to help individuals expand their *psychological flexibility* by learning to acknowledge and accept their thoughts and emotions as they are. Rather than allowing negative thoughts and emotions to define who the individual is, ACT allows people to view them as passing feelings that come and go in the moment.

It seems to me that ACT is dismissive of feelings

If this book is your first encounter with Acceptance and Commitment Therapy, or other acceptance-based approaches, it could seem like unpleasant emotions or painful emotions are not taken seriously. In reality, I would argue that the opposite is true.

ACT encourages you to genuinely feel your emotions. Don't resist them, or hide from them. Feel your feelings, learn from them and accept them. Then take the next step in your valued direction.

One thing that ACT (and Morita therapy) does do is refuse to let emotions run the show. You are not a prisoner to your emotions, or unable to act until you have removed all unpleasant feelings.

Isn't experiential avoidance natural?

Quite possibly. However, I can think of all kinds of actions that might be considered 'natural,' but would not seem like a beneficial choice for most people in the 21st century.

A more relevant question might be, "Is experiential avoidance useful in getting where I want to go?"

How do I stop focusing on feelings?

By focusing on something else!

If you try to force yourself not to focus on feelings, you are likely to obsess about that at some level and make your feelings even bigger and stronger.

Instead, welcome the feelings. Get to know them – and then allow them to motivate you along your valued path.

What does EFT have to do with Acceptance?

EFT may be thought of as an example of kinaesthetic hypnosis.

Regardless of any meridian points or suchlike, EFT seems to work because the added somatic element helps those clients who are perhaps less inclined to function intellectually. That is, the added physical element allows clients to take on board the spoken affirmations.

The words spoken during an EFT session are not insignificant:

> Even though [fill-in issue statement], I love and accept myself completely.

> Example: Even though I worry about my teenage daughter, I love and accept myself completely.

It can therefore be seen that the core of EFT is a bodily experience of acceptance.

Tapping does not depend on acceptance

We have not suggested that all tapping methods "depend" on acceptance. We have simply demonstrated that as far as EFT is concerned, acceptance plays a central role.

Having said that, if you look at other tapping methods, even those that do not use any kind of statement, I am confident that you will be able to find acceptance as a vital part of the mechanism.

All of the tapping systems that I am aware of involve focusing on your unpleasant feelings, or experiences, whilst you also focus on the physical tapping. This means that acceptance – understood as starting where you are – is essential to the method.

What do you really think of Byron Katie and The Work?

We don't know Byron Katie personally, so are in no

position to comment on her as a person. 'The Work,' which is what Katie calls her method of self-inquiry, has been experienced as a useful tool by many people. The ideas contained within are certainly not original, but the way they are worded – including what is said and what is not said – make it a useful process.

After asking the four questions of The Work, you are provided with a 'turnaround.' This is simply an invitation to look at your issue from a number of different perspectives. It is potentially a very powerful climax to the process, but should be handled with care. If someone is facing trauma or emotionally vulnerable, there is a risk that the turnaround could lead to the acceptance of potentially unhelpful thoughts. Instead, it should be remembered, that The Work is not seeking to reveal the 'truth' of a situation, but helping you find a way to accept and engage with reality. If the turnaround you come up with leaves you in a worse condition than the initial issue being worked-on, keep going until you come up with something else.

Does The Work teach that we should just accept reality as it is?

The following answer is taken from the official website for The Work:

> The Work doesn't say what anyone *should* or

shouldn't do. We simply ask: What is the effect of arguing with reality? How does it feel? This Work explores the cause and effect of attaching to painful thoughts, and in that investigation we find our freedom. To simply say that we *shouldn't* argue with reality is just to add another story, another philosophy or religion. It hasn't ever worked.

CHAPTER SIXTEEN

Where do we go from here?

Well, onward in our valued direction, obviously!

If you have found the ideas in this book intriguing or helpful in any way, you might want to consider some of the following options along this liberating road of acceptance.

Look out for acceptance – everywhere!

Have you ever noticed what happens when you buy a new car? Without even trying to, you almost always begin noticing your make or colour of car *everywhere*!

I once bought a car that I had not previously heard of and had never seen on the road. Yet, that same day I saw about a dozen of them!

Once you are aware of and focused on something, it becomes almost impossible not to see it everywhere you look. The same is true of acceptance.

Carl Jung, the famous Swiss psychiatrist, wrote, 'We cannot change anything until we accept it. Condemnation does not liberate, it oppresses.'

George Orwell once wrote that, 'Happiness can exist only in acceptance.'

Lao Tzu, the founder of philosophical Taoism, wrote that, 'Life is a series of natural and spontaneous changes. Don't resist them; that only creates sorrow. Let reality be reality. Let things flow naturally forward in whatever way they like.'

According to Bryant McGill, 'Acceptance is the road to all change.'

The revered psychologist, Carl Rogers, stated that, 'The curious paradox is that when I accept myself just as I am, then I can change.'

Paulo Coelho, author of *The Alchemist*, tells us that, 'It's best to accept life as it really is and not as I imagined it to be.'

Tara Brach, author of *Radical Acceptance*, writes that, 'There is something wonderfully bold and liberating about saying yes to our entire imperfect and messy life.'

As you can see, acceptance is everywhere! It crops up in almost all schools of psychology and psychotherapy at some point. It can be found in all of the major religions of the world. It is emphasised by countless personal development teachers.

It is talked about all over the place. The challenge for us now is to move beyond talk and start living it!

Check out Constructive Living

I would encourage anyone interested in the Morita Therapy approach to acceptance to read David K. Reynolds' *Constructive Living*. Reynolds has perhaps done more to bring Morita Therapy (along with other Japanese therapies) to the West than anyone else.

Explore ACT

If you would like to explore a thorough approach to acceptance, you cannot go far wrong with Acceptance and Commitment Therapy. I have listed a number of books that you might want to check out below.

Consider Radical Acceptance

If you find ACT a bit heavy (and there's no reason why you should), you might want to read Tara Brach's book, *Radical Acceptance*. It is more 'spiritual' than other books and methods I recommend, but it is easy enough to read past those bits, if you prefer. Nevertheless, Brach's book contains page after page of gems regarding the benefits of acceptance and how to apply them to your life.

You may also enjoy some of her talks on YouTube.

Visit the Brief Acceptance website

If you want to learn more about Brief Acceptance methods, as well as getting your hands on some free resources, you can visit:

www.briefacceptance.com/letitbe

Further Reading:

The following books may be of interest.

ACT

The Happiness Trap by Russ Harris

Things Might Go Terribly Horribly Wrong by Kelly Wilson

A Liberated Mind by Steven Hayes

Get Out of Your Mind and Into Your Life by Steven Hayes

DBT

DBT Skills Workbook by Sheri Van Dijk

Calming the Emotional Storm by Sheri Van Dijk

Morita Therapy

Natural Path to Wellness by Gregg Krech

Rivers to Live By by Brian Ogawa

Constructive Living by David K. Reynolds

The Work

Loving What Is by Byron Katie

The Option Method

The Myth of Unhappiness, Vol. 1, by Bruce di Marsico

Unlock Your Happiness with Five Simple Questions by Bruce di Marsico

EFT

The Tapping Solution: A Revolutionary System for Stress-Free Living by Nick Ortner

The Science Behind Tapping by Peta Stapleton

General

Radical Acceptance by Tara Brach

Sane New World by Ruby Wax

Full-catastrophe Living by Jon Kabat-Zinn

The Way of Effortless Mindfulness by Loch Kelly

Man's Search for Meaning by Viktor Frankl

The Lost Art of Being Happy: Spirituality for Sceptics by Tony Wilkinson

The Subtle Art Of Not Giving a Fuck by Mark Manson

Living Life On Purpose by Matthew McKay, John Forsyth, and Georg Eifert

Finally...

It has been my joy to share the Brief Acceptance method(s) and mindset with you. If you skimmed through this book – and, of course, we've all done it at times – I would now encourage you to go back and give it a second read. You will get the most out of *Let it Be* if you carry out the exercises and practice everything that the book invites you to do.

Thanks for getting this far. Please feel free to contact me with any questions or stories related to the liberating road of Brief Acceptance.

Bibliography

Allione, Tsultrim. (2008.) *Feeding Your Demons - Ancient Wisdom for Resolving Inner Conflict.* London: Hay House.

Brach, T. (2004.) *Radical Acceptance.* New York: Random House.

Brantley, J., McKay, M., Wood, J., (2019.) *The Dialectical Behaviour Therapy Skills Workbook.* Oakland, CA: New Harbinger Publications.

Corsini, R., (2001.) *Handbook of Innovative Psychotherapies.* New York: J. Wiley.

Dijk, S., (2012.) *Calming the Emotional Storm: Using Dialectical Behavior Therapy Skills to Manage Your Emotions and Balance Your Life.* Oakland, CA: New

Harbinger Publications.

Dijk, S., (2012.) *DBT Made Simple.* Oakland, CA: New Harbinger Publications.

Ellis, A. and Joffe-Ellis, D., (2019.) *Rational Emotive Behavior Therapy.* Washington, DC: American Psychological Association.

Fisher, P. and Wells, A., 2010. *Metacognitive Therapy.* London: Routledge.

Fujita, C., (1986.) *Morita therapy.* Tokyo: Igaku-Shoin.

Hayes, Steven, C., (2005) *Get out of your mind and into your life.* Oakland, CA: New Harbinger.

Hayes, Steven, C., (2019.) *A Liberated Mind.* London: Vermillion.

Hill, J. and Oliver, J., (2019.) *Acceptance and Commitment Coaching.* Abingdon: Routledge.

Kabat-Zinn, J., (1991.) *Full catastrophe living.* New York: Delta.

Katie, B., (2002.) *Loving what is.* New York: Harmony Books.

Kelly, Loch. (2019.) *The Way of Effortless Mindfulness.* Boulder, CO: Sounds True.

Krech, Gregg. (2015.) *A Natural Approach to Mental Wellness: Japanese Psychology and the Skills We Need for*

Psychological and Spiritual Health. Vermont: ToDo Institute.

Krech, Gregg. (2014.) *The Art of Taking Action: Lessons from Japanese Psychology*. Vermont: ToDo Institute.

Manson, M. (2016) *The Subtle art of not giving a fuck*. New York: HarperCollins

Marsico, Bruce. (2006.) *The Option Method: Unlock Your Happiness With Five Simple Questions. Walnut Grove, CA: Dragonfly Press.*

Marsico, Bruce. (2010.) *The Myth of Unhappiness, Vol. 1.* Montclair, NJ*:* Dialogues in Self Discovery.

McKay, M., Forsyth, J. and Eifert, G., (2010.) *Your life on Purpose*. Oakland, CA: New Harbinger Publications.

Morita, Shoma. (1998.) *Morita Therapy and the True Nature of Anxiety-Based Disorders (Shinkeishitsu)*. New York: SUNY.

Ogawa, Brian. (2007.) *A River to Live By: The 12 Principles of Morita Therapy*. Hawaii: Xlibris.

Ogawa, Brian. (2013.) *Desire For Life: The Practitioner's Introduction to Morita Therapy for the Treatment of Anxiety Disorders.* Hawaii: Xlibris.

Reynolds, David. (1984.) *Constructive Living*. Hawaii: Kolowalu.

Reynolds, David. (1982.) *The Quiet Therapies*: Japanese

Pathways to Personal Growth. Hawaii: UPOH.

Reynolds, David. (1995.) *A Handbook for Constructive Living.* New York: William Morris & Co.

Roemer, L. and Orsillo, S. (2010.) *Mindfulness and Acceptance Based Behavioral Therapies in Practice.* New York: The Guildford Press.

Siegel, Ronald, D. (2010.) *The Mindfulness Solution.* New York: The Guildford Press.

Wax, R., (2013.) *Sane New World.* London: Hodder & Stoughton.

About the Author

Graham Old is a Solution-focused therapist, hypnotist and author from the United Kingdom. He has experience as an Assistant Social Worker and a Father's Worker, as well as working in private practice and running one of the most popular hypnosis sites on the web.

Graham is a popular international speaker, writer and trainer, with over two decades experience teaching meditation and self-hypnosis. He is an innovative presence in contemporary hypnosis and the developer of the popular 'Therapeutic Inductions' approach.

www.briefacceptance.com

www.plasticspoonbooks.com

Printed in Great Britain
by Amazon